CLASSICS IN EDUCATION
Lawrence A. Cremin, General Editor

☆ ☆ ☆

THE REPUBLIC AND THE SCHOOL
Horace Mann on the Education of Free Men
Edited by Lawrence A. Cremin

AMERICAN IDEAS ABOUT ADULT EDUCATION
1710–1951
Edited by C. Hartley Grattan

DEWEY ON EDUCATION
Introduction and Notes by Martin S. Dworkin

THE SUPREME COURT AND EDUCATION
Edited by David Fellman

INTERNATIONAL EDUCATION
A Documentary History
Edited by David G. Scanlon

CRUSADE AGAINST IGNORANCE
Thomas Jefferson on Education
Edited by Gordon C. Lee

CHINESE EDUCATION UNDER COMMUNISM
Edited by Chang-tu Hu

CHARLES W. ELIOT AND POPULAR EDUCATION
Edited by Edward A. Krug

WILLIAM T. HARRIS ON EDUCATION
(in preparation)
Edited by Martin S. Dworkin

THE *EMILE* OF JEAN JACQUES ROUSSEAU
Selections
Translated and Edited by William Boyd

THE MINOR EDUCATIONAL WRITINGS OF
JEAN JACQUES ROUSSEAU
Selected and Translated by William Boyd

PSYCHOLOGY AND THE SCIENCE OF EDUCATION
Selected Writings of Edward L. Thorndike
Edited by Geraldine M. Joncich

THE NEW-ENGLAND PRIMER
Introduction by Paul Leicester Ford

BENJAMIN FRANKLIN ON EDUCATION
Edited by John Hardin Best

THE COLLEGES AND THE PUBLIC
1787–1862
Edited by Theodore Rawson Crane

TRADITIONS OF AFRICAN EDUCATION
Edited by David G. Scanlon

NOAH WEBSTER'S AMERICAN SPELLING BOOK
Introductory Essay by Henry Steele Commager

VITTORINO DA FELTRE
AND OTHER HUMANIST EDUCATORS
By William Harrison Woodward
Foreword by Eugene F. Rice, Jr.

DESIDERIUS ERASMUS
CONCERNING THE AIM AND METHOD
OF EDUCATION
By William Harrison Woodward
Foreword by Craig R. Thompson

JOHN LOCKE ON EDUCATION
Edited by Peter Gay

CATHOLIC EDUCATION IN AMERICA
A Documentary History
Edited by Neil G. McCluskey, S.J.

THE AGE OF THE ACADEMIES
Edited by Theodore R. Sizer

HEALTH, GROWTH, AND HEREDITY
G. Stanley Hall on Natural Education
Edited by Charles E. Strickland and Charles Burgess

TEACHER EDUCATION IN AMERICA
A Documentary History
Edited by Merle L. Borrowman

THE EDUCATED WOMAN IN AMERICA
Selected Writings of Catharine Beecher,
Margaret Fuller, and M. Carey Thomas
Edited by Barbara M. Cross

EMERSON ON EDUCATION
Selections
Edited by Howard Mumford Jones

ECONOMIC INFLUENCES UPON EDUCATIONAL
PROGRESS IN THE UNITED STATES, 1820–1850
By Frank Tracy Carlton
Foreword by Lawrence A. Cremin

QUINTILIAN ON EDUCATION
Selected and Translated by William M. Smail

ROMAN EDUCATION FROM CICERO
TO QUINTILIAN
By Aubrey Gwynn, S.J.

HERBERT SPENCER ON EDUCATION
Edited by Andreas M. Kazamias

JOHN LOCKE'S *OF THE CONDUCT OF THE UNDERSTANDING*
Edited by Francis W. Garforth

STUDIES IN EDUCATION DURING THE AGE OF THE RENAISSANCE, 1400–1600
By William Harrison Woodward
Foreword by Lawrence Stone

JOHN AMOS COMENIUS ON EDUCATION
Introduction by Jean Piaget

HUMANISM AND THE SOCIAL ORDER IN TUDOR ENGLAND
By Fritz Caspari

VIVES' *INTRODUCTION TO WISDOM*
Edited by Marian Leona Tobriner, S.N.J.M.

THE THEORY OF EDUCATION IN THE *REPUBLIC* OF PLATO
By Richard Lewis Nettleship
Foreword by Robert McClintock

UTOPIANISM AND EDUCATION
Robert Owen and the Owenites
Edited by John F. C. Harrison

Utopianism and Education

ROBERT OWEN AND THE OWENITES

Edited, with an Introduction and Notes, by
JOHN F. C. HARRISON

CLASSICS IN

No. 37

EDUCATION

TEACHERS COLLEGE PRESS
TEACHERS COLLEGE, COLUMBIA UNIVERSITY
NEW YORK

© 1968 by Teachers College
Columbia University

Library of Congress Catalog
Card Number 68-54675

Manufactured in the United States of America

Foreword

The communitarian experiments of the nineteenth century, Arthur Bestor pointed out some years ago, have always held a unique appeal for Americans, dedicated as they have been to the institutionalizing of revolution. On the one hand, communities such as Mount Lebanon in New York, Nashoba in Tennessee, and New Harmony in Indiana, were able to exemplify truly radical departures from traditional social and economic relationships; on the other hand, they were able to proceed in a peaceful, orderly manner, the assumption being that the larger society had only to see the model at work before proceeding to initiate its own reforms. Thus, communitarianism could at the same time symbolize meliorism and revolution to a people who were deeply committed to both by sentiment and by tradition.

The sources of the several experiments were as various as the men and women who undertook them. Some, like Mormonism, sprang from indigenous roots, growing up during the widespread sectarian enthusiasm of the 1820's and 1830's; others, like Shakerism, traced their origins to England or the Continent. Similarly, while some were patently religious in inspiration, others, like Fourierism, were much more political and economic in character. Owenism, of course, was one of the latter, taking form as it did in New Lanark, Scotland, and later being transplanted to New Harmony, Indiana. Indeed, as Professor Harrison quite rightly suggests, one of the most fascinating things about Owenism was its attractiveness to societies as different as early industrial England and agricultural frontier America.

From the beginning, Owenism cast education as a central instrument of reform, maintaining that long-range social improvement depended on more profound understanding and more careful control of the processes of character formation. That alone would render the movement worthy of systematic study by students of educational history. But in light of the characteristic American propensity to seek reform through education, Owenism takes on added significance as an important source of the dominant political tradition. And, as such, it merits the close attention of all who would comprehend both the strengths and weaknesses of the American political system in dealing with problems of pressing social concern.

LAWRENCE A. CREMIN

Contents

INTRODUCTION
   by *John F. C. Harrison*   1

1. Robert Owen: A New View of Society   41
2. Robert Owen: The Institution for the Formation of Character   80
3. Robert Owen: Rational Education for the New World   118
4. Robert Dale Owen: Education at New Lanark   129
5. Robert Owen: Ten Rules for an Infant School   173
6. Jane Dale Owen: The Principles of Natural Education   176
7. Abram Combe: The Definition of Education   189
8. William Thompson: Education in a Community   196
9. William Maclure: Opinions on Various Subjects   231

Utopianism and Education
ROBERT OWEN AND THE OWENITES

Introduction

By JOHN F. C. HARRISON

The inscription on Robert Owen's monument in Kensal Green Cemetery, London, begins: "He originated and organized infant schools." This claim, although disputed during his lifetime, is now generally acknowledged and has become part of the familiar story of Owen. However, for fifty years after his death in 1858 Owen was remembered chiefly as a cooperator, secularist, and utopian socialist, and Frank Podmore in his definitive biography of Owen published in 1906 observed that "the name of Robert Owen is little known to the present generation as an educational reformer."[1] Thanks to Podmore's work and, later, that of another Fabian, G. D. H. Cole, Owen's role as an educator became more fully recognized.[2] Subsequent biographies and educational dissertations elaborated (or, perhaps more accurately, repeated) details of

[1] Frank Podmore, *Robert Owen: A Biography*, 2 vols. (London, 1906), I, 102.

[2] G. D. H. Cole, *Robert Owen* (London, 1925); and Cole's introduction to his edition of Owen, *A New View of Society and Other Writings* (London, 1927). Other Fabians also wrote on Owen, notably Margaret Cole, B. L. Hutchins, Sidney and Beatrice Webb, Graham Wallas, and C. E. M. Joad. The following recent studies of Owen include descriptions of his educational experiments and principles: Rowland Hill Harvey, *Robert Owen, Social Idealist* (Berkeley and Los Angeles, 1949); Margaret Cole, *Robert Owen of New Lanark* (London, 1953); A. L. Morton, *The Life and Ideas of Robert Owen* (London, 1962); Harold Silver, *The Concept of Popular Education* (London, 1965).

Owen's educational activities and ideas. More recently Arthur Eugene Bestor, through a brilliant examination of the American material, showed the close relationship between education and Owenite communitarianism.[3]

In modern evaluations of Owen and his work a large place has thus been rightly accorded to education. The spectacular nature of the experiment at New Lanark, the advocacy of a nonviolent and widely acceptable method of social change, and Owen's repeated emphasis on the importance of education in character formation, all contributed to a focusing of attention on this aspect of his achievement. Owen's statements on the relation between education and social reform, and descriptions of the detailed workings of his infant school, strengthened the impression that the basis of Owenism was educational. His first important work, *A New View of Society*, was in one sense a general treatise on education.

For the most part studies of Owenite education have been concerned with the institutions at New Lanark and New Harmony, or with the educational theories of Owen himself. But it is probably now more fruitful to treat educational history in broader terms, as sociointellectual history, and to draw on the writings of Owen's followers as well as on Owen's works. In order to get beyond the familiar account of Owen's views on infant schools and character formation (or perhaps, rather, to see these in perspective), Owenism has to be approached as a body of social thought which was rooted in the late eighteenth and early nineteenth centuries and which can be broken

[3] Arthur Eugene Bestor, Jr., *Backwoods Utopias: The Sectarian and Owenite Phases of Communitarian Socialism in America, 1663–1829* (Philadelphia, 1950); and Bestor, *Education and Reform at New Harmony: Correspondence of William Maclure and Marie Duclos Fretageot, 1820–1833.* Indiana Historical Society (Indianapolis, 1948).

down into its constituent parts for analysis. Each of these parts can be shown to have some educational content; and when the interlocking and reinforcing nature of the parts is demonstrated the strength of the educational element in Owenism becomes explicable. What emerges is the working out of Owenism in educational terms.

The history of Robert Owen and the movement associated with his name has produced a considerable literature. In Britain, Owen has been accorded a niche in the standard histories of British labor and socialism, and the usual treatment of Owenism in recent years has been as a phase in the history of the British working-class movement[4]—a link in the continuous chain which is traced from 1789 to the Wilson government. In America the emphasis has been different. Here Owenism has been treated as part of the communitarian tradition by historians from John Humphrey Noyes to Arthur Eugene Bestor. The standard accounts present it as an episode in the quest for utopia or as an aspect of "freedom's ferment."[5] New Harmony has also exercised a continuing fascination for essayists, novelists, and writers of semi-serious history.

Until recently no attempt was made to comprehend the whole of the Owenite record, putting the British and the American material together and searching for an interpretation of Owenism in relation to the two different societies.[6] If we set aside the various partial interpreta-

[4] For example, G. D. H. Cole, *A Short History of the British Working-Class Movement, 1789–1947* (London, revised ed., 1948).
[5] For example, John Humphrey Noyes, *History of American Socialisms* (New York, 1870; repr., 1961); George B. Lockwood, *The New Harmony Movement* (New York, 1905); Alice Felt Tyler, *Freedom's Ferment* (1944; repr., New York, 1962).
[6] This is the theme of J. F. C. Harrison, *Quest for the New Moral World: Robert Owen and the Owenites in Britain and America*

tions the central feature of Owenism is the dual nature of its role in two such different societies as early industrial Britain and agricultural, frontier America. That contemporaries should have considered Owenite ideas and institutions relevant in these two very different contexts is the starting point for new questions and new approaches. Instead of asking what Owenism contributed to the making of the English working class, or how it related to American frontier conditions and westward expansion, we have to examine the points of contact or similarity in British and American social experience which made Owenism acceptable in certain situations.

The interrelationship of the British and American Owenite movements is demonstrated most obviously by their chronology. Owen's first Essay on the Formation of Character, setting forth his *New View of Society*, appeared in London in 1813; and in the summer of 1817 he launched his first great propaganda campaign. From then until 1824 Owen's schemes were continually before the public eye in Britain, but did not attract much attention elsewhere. In the fall of 1824, however, he shifted the scene of his operations to the New World, and early in 1825 launched his first community at New Harmony in Indiana. His Scottish followers at the same time began the first British Owenite community at Orbiston in Lanarkshire. The developments on both sides of the Atlantic were regarded as parts of the same movement, and news of the communities and proposed communities was exchanged regularly. About ten Owenite communities were founded in North America in the 1820's but none of them lasted more than two or three years,[7] and

---

(London and New York, 1968), which provides documentation for the statements made in this essay. There is also a full bibliography.
[7] New Harmony, Indiana (1825-28); Yellow Springs Community,

by 1829 the first phase of Owenism in America came to an end. In Britain, attempts to organize stable communities in the 1820's were similarly frustrated, but out of these efforts emerged a new type of Owenite institution—the cooperative trading association. From 1828 cooperative stores increased rapidly and by 1830 the *Cooperator* claimed that three hundred existed in the United Kingdom. On his return from America in 1829 Owen discovered a considerable working-class interest in his ideas, and from then until 1834 Owenism captured the imagination of many proletarian leaders. First through the National Equitable Labour Exchange, and then through the Grand National Consolidated Trades Union, Owen for a time emerged as the leader of the laboring poor. But these institutions collapsed in 1834 and Owenism in Britain entered a new phase, signaled by the appearance of the journal, the *New Moral World*.[8] The Owenite movement of the 1834-1845 period was characterized by renewed efforts to found communities, and by the building of an organization of local branches throughout the Kingdom. Five communities were launched,[9] and Halls

---

Ohio (1825-26); Franklin Community, Haverstraw, New York (1826-28); Forestville Community, Coxsackie, New York (1826-27); Kendall Community, Ohio (1826-28); Valley Forge Community, Pennsylvania (1826); Wanborough Cooperative Association (1825); Blue Spring Community, Indiana (1826-27); Nashoba, Tennessee (1826-28); Maxwell Community, Ontario, Canada (1827).

[8] The main Owenite journals covering the history of the movement were the *Economist* (1821-22); the *New Harmony Gazette* (1825-28), continued as the *Free Enquirer* (1828-35); the *Cooperative Magazine* (1826-30); the *Crisis* (1832-34); the *New Moral World* (1834-45); the *Herald of Progress* (1845-46); and the *Reasoner* (1846-72).

[9] The British communities were: Orbiston, Lanarkshire (1825-27); Devonshire Community, Exeter (1826-27); Ralahine, County Clare, Ireland (1831-33); Pant Glas, Merionethshire, Wales (1840); Manea Fen, Cambridgeshire (1838-40); Harmony Hall (Queenwood),

of Science were opened in the larger towns. In America there was no comparable movement to build a local branch organization, but in the general communitarian revival of the 1840's three Owenite communities were started, and Owenite influence was strong in at least two others.[10] As an organized movement Owenism was dead in both countries after 1848, but an Owenite legacy was carried by old Owenites into later movements such as secularism, consumers' cooperation, associationism, and spiritualism.

Throughout its thirty-year history the Owenite movement has thus to be traced in both Britain and America. A certain unity, especially in the 1820's, was imposed by the domination of Robert Owen himself, and also by the strong fraternal interest which English Owenites had in American communitarian experiments in general. Owenites largely ignored the differences between American and British society and tended to think of a common pattern of social development for both countries. The principles of Owenism were considered as universally valid irrespective of time and place. Nevertheless, Owenite concepts and institutions did in fact differ in the two countries. Some elements in the British Owenite tradition were entirely lacking or greatly weakened in the American movement and, conversely, Owenism in America carried overtones which were not present in Britain. These differences had a reacting and reinforcing effect on what appeared to be a common core of beliefs and institutional experiences.

Tytherly, Hampshire (1839–45); Garnlwyd, Carmarthenshire, Wales (1847–55).

[10] The Owenite communities were the Society of One-Mentians, Pennsylvania (1843–44); Goose Pond Community, Pennsylvania (1843); and Equality, Wisconsin (1843–46). Owenite influence was apparent also in Skaneateles Community, New York (1843–46), and in Utopia, Ohio (1847).

MR. OWEN'S NEW VIEW OF SOCIETY

When Robert Owen wrote his *New View of Society* in 1812-1813 he was forty-two years of age, and already famed as one of the outstandingly successful businessmen of the age. The story of his youth and early experiences in Manchester and New Lanark has been told many times, although nowhere better than in his own engaging autobiography, published at the end of his life.[11] According to his own account he began his "mission to openly propagate my 'new views of society'" in the summer of 1802,[12] but it was not until 1813 that he began to formulate his views in print. For the next forty-five years a constant stream of books, pamphlets, periodicals, and letters to the press flowed from his pen, repeating and elaborating his doctrines. From this mass of material three works stand out as containing, between them, a fairly comprehensive statement of Owen's theories. *A New View of Society; or essays on the principle of the formation of the human character* stands in the same relation to Owenism as the *Communist Manifesto* does to Marxism—the earliest statement by the master of his doctrines, containing in embryo all the ideas which were to be developed further in later works. In his *Report to the County of Lanark* (1821) Owen formulated his communitarian doctrines; and in the *Book of the New Moral World* (1836-1844) he drew together his theoretical writings on the social sciences.

The active dissemination of his new view of society

---

[11] *Life of Robert Owen, Written by Himself*, 2 vols., numbered I and IA (London, 1857-58). This contains appendixes in which Owen reprinted his chief publications up to 1821. References to these writings are taken from this collection, and cited as Owen, *Life*.

[12] Owen, *Life*, I, 76.

drew to Owen his first followers. He sent copies of *A New View of Society* to all the governments in Europe and America and to leading British public figures. He had an interview with the prime minister, Lord Liverpool, to discuss it. In the summer of 1817 he embarked on an intensive propaganda, deluging the newspapers with texts of his addresses which they printed in full. He spent four thousand pounds in two months and made himself a nationally known figure. Looking back on his life, it seemed to Owen that 1817 marked the great turning point in his career. In this year he busied himself with working out a solution to urgent problems of poor relief which, after presentation at public meetings and in various committees, finally emerged as a fully fledged proposal of communitarianism in the *Report to the County of Lanark*.

The first Owenites who were attracted by these views between 1817 and 1824 indicate clearly the nature of Owen's appeal. A strong Scottish element attested the local influence of New Lanark: Archibald James Hamilton of Dalziel, Abram Combe of Edinburgh, and Captain Donald Macdonald.[13] Second, a group of philanthropists

---

[13] Archibald James Hamilton (1793–1834), the son of the laird of Dalziel and Orbiston, was a lieutenant in the Scots Greys at Waterloo. He became an ardent follower of Owen, and was associated with Abram Combe in the Orbiston community experiment, for which he provided the land.

Abram Combe (1785–1827) was the son of an Edinburgh brewer, and the brother of George Combe, the phrenologist. He made a prosperous living as a tanner and in 1821 became a convert to Owenism. After establishing an Owenite society known as the Edinburgh Practical Society (1821–22), he published several works on Owenism (1823–25), and in 1825 launched (with A. J. Hamilton) the Orbiston community.

Donald Macdonald (1791–1872) was a captain in the Royal Engineers, and while stationed in Edinburgh became interested in Owenism and joined the Edinburgh Practical Society. He accom-

(gentlemen and businessmen) of independent means, such as John Minter Morgan, William Thompson, and John Gray, combined Owen's views with their own schemes for social reform.[14] And a third group, led by George Mudie and Henry Hetherington, constituted a working-class response among some London printers.[15]

---

panied Owen on his tour of Ireland in 1822-23 and went with him to America on his first journey in 1824. He made a second journey to America in 1825-26 and was active in the New Harmony community.

[14] John Minter Morgan (1782-1854) inherited "an ample fortune" from his father, a wholesale stationer of London, and spent his life pursuing philanthropic interests. As early as 1819 he published a defence of Owen's views, and his *Revolt of the Bees* (London, 1826) was one of the most widely read of the popularizations of Owenism. He was a member of the Church of England and sought to reconcile his Christian beliefs with Owenite community projects.

William Thompson (1775-1833), an Irish landowner, identified himself completely with the Owenite movement, and developed the fullest exposition of Ricardian-Owenite socialism. As a young man he was influenced by the French Revolution, and was later a friend of Jeremy Bentham. In addition to his Benthamite and Owenist interests he was also a champion of women's rights. For an exposition of Ricardian socialism see M. Beer, *A History of British Socialism* (London, 1948), Part II.

John Gray (1799-1883) joined a "large manufacturing and wholesale house" in London at the age of fourteen and subsequently had a prosperous commercial career. He intended to join the Orbiston community but withdrew and published a criticism of it. His *Lecture on Human Happiness* (London, 1825) was a defence of Owenism and Ricardian socialism, although he never accepted all Owen's theories. From 1832 he repudiated his earlier connections with Owenism and devoted himself to plans for monetary reform.

[15] George Mudie, a Scots journalist and printer, came to London about 1820. He was already familiar with Owen's views and in January 1821 he started a weekly journal, the *Economist*, to promote Owenism. In the same year he established a Practical and Economical Society, which started an experiment in cooperative housing in Spa Fields, London. He probably joined the Orbiston community, and in the 1840's was still active as a social reformer.

Henry Hetherington (1792-1849) served his apprenticeship with Luke Hansard, the parliamentary printer. He was active in prac-

At various points these groups overlapped, both institutionally and in their ideas. In America Owen's new view of society did not make much headway until his arrival in November 1824, after which the links between the American and British Owenites became close. However, about 1820 Cornelius Camden Blatchly founded the New York Society for Promoting Communities, and quoted Owen in his *Essay on Common Wealths* (1822).[16] In Philadelphia a small group of Owenites among the membership of the Academy of Natural Sciences included Dr. Gerard Troost, John Speakman, and William Maclure.[17] These various followers of Owen soon supplemented his theories with views of their own. They tended to treat Owen's work eclectically, each adding something and omitting what he did not like. Thus there emerged a body of social thought distinctively Owenist in content, but not confined within the writings of Robert Owen. A concern for education was central to all presentations of Owenism, although the amount and direction of emphasis varied between different groups and periods.

---

tically all the great working-class agitations from the 1820's to the 1840's—Chartism, trade unionism, secularism—but was best known for his part in the struggle for the unstamped press, in which his paper, the *Poor Man's Guardian,* was central. He was imprisoned several times for his publishing activities and was a lifelong Owenite.

[16] Cornelius Camden Blatchly was a New York physician and member of the Society of Friends. He had originally reached a social philosophy similar to but indepedent of that of Owen; and after reading *A New View of Society* he welcomed it as confirmation of his own views.

[17] Bestor, *Backwoods Utopias,* p. 100. William Maclure (1763–1840) was a Scottish merchant who acquired a fortune and then retired to pursue his educational and scientific interests. He moved to Philadelphia and became an American citizen. He was in contact with the leading scientific figures of the age, and experimented with Pestalozzian schools in Philadelphia. From his educational work he was led into more general schemes for social reform.

It has been customary to consider Owenite education as a more or less self-contained element in Owenism, sometimes to present it as the central core around which other aspects were wrapped. At times Owen himself spoke in terms suggestive of these interpretations, and in most places the school remained the most enduring part of the local institutions of Owenism. Nevertheless, Owenism was not primarily a movement to found schools and literary institutes; it was a new view of society whose adherents wanted a radical transformation of the economic and social structure which they believed could be effected in accordance with the laws of social science. The place of education in this scheme of social change becomes clear in the first instance through an analysis of the constituents of Owenism.

Like all social theories, Owenism was a complex of ideas drawn from several sources united within an overall intellectual framework. This was based on certain underlying assumptions which contemporaries rarely mentioned because they either took them for granted or were simply unaware of them. One need not doubt Owen's honesty in his claim that his views were entirely original and owed nothing to previous thinkers, but his claim cannot be taken at its face value. The origin of his ideas has perplexed most of his biographers, for they could find little evidence of any formative reading and his son had stated that his father seldom read books. A possible clue has been sought in the intellectual influence which membership in the Manchester Literary and Philosophical Society in the 1790's might have had on him.[18] To a young man in his early twenties these con-

[18] See E. M. Fraser, "Robert Owen in Manchester, 1787-1800," in *Memoirs and Proceedings of the Manchester Literary and Philosophical Society*, LXXXII (1937-38), 29-41.

tacts with individual members were undoubtedly stimulating, but direct links with his later ideas seem somewhat tenuous. In any case, the pedigree of ideas can seldom be traced like a single line of issue in a family tree. And the starting point is not Manchester but Scotland.

The intellectual renaissance in Scotland in the second half of the eighteenth century produced a notable school of moral philosophers and political economists who were concerned to establish "an empirical basis for the study of man and society."[19] In their discussions of human nature, social forces and institutions, economic processes, and government—all included in the omnibus category, moral philosophy—there emerged the beginnings of modern sociology and the idea of social science. At the universities of Edinburgh and Glasgow the teaching and discussion of moral philosophy nurtured a school of what a later age would label the behavioral sciences. Into this atmosphere Robert Owen moved in 1800. He married the daughter of David Dale, a religiously minded Scots merchant and industrialist, and made his home in Scotland for a quarter of a century, at first spending the summers in a cottage in New Lanark and the winters in Glasgow, and later living at Braxfield House, New Lanark. His fortune and his fame were made by the banks of the Clyde. He was a member of the Glasgow Literary and Commercial Society, and states that he "was on the most

[19] Gladys Bryson, *Man and Society: The Scottish Inquiry of the Eighteenth Century* (Princeton, 1945), p. 1. This Scottish group included David Hume, Francis Hutcheson, Adam Smith, Thomas Reid, Adam Ferguson, Dugald Stewart, Lord Kames (Henry Home), Lord Monboddo (James Burnet). See also William C. Lehmann, *John Millar of Glasgow, 1735–1801* (Cambridge, 1960); and Ronald L. Meek, "The Scottish Contribution to Marxist Sociology," in John Saville, ed., *Democracy and the Labour Movement* (London, 1954), pp. 84–102.

friendly terms with many of the professors of the universities of Edinburgh and Glasgow.[20] Among his friends were James Mill, Patrick Colquhoun, and Lord Kames. About 1813 he began more deliberately to widen his circle of contacts.

In his writings Owen seldom quoted any other author, since he was convinced that his views sprang entirely from his own experience in Manchester and, more particularly, at New Lanark. Yet the terminology he uses, the assumptions he makes, and the particular way he approaches problems are in the tradition of the Scottish Enlightenment. In his followers the same characteristics are evident, and in addition they did not hesitate to cite authors, such as Dugald Stewart, whom they thought would strengthen their case. Through "the Scottish inquiry of the eighteenth century" the ideas of the Enlightenment were mediated to the Owenites. But it was the fate of Owenism to be caught between the Enlightenment of the eighteenth century and the Romantic reaction to it; and Owen, like William Godwin (with whose *Political Justice* [1793] there is considerable similarity), sought to assimilate elements of both.

The beginning of Owenite argument was always the premise of happiness. Man's fundamental motivation was the pursuit of his own happiness, which could, however, only be fully attained through the promotion of the happiness of the community. The sole end of society, of government, and of all human relations was the promotion of the maximum amount of happiness for the greatest possible number. By this criterion it was very clear that there must be something wrong with contemporary society, for nothing was more obvious than

[20] Owen, *Life*, I, 107.

that a majority of people did not enjoy much happiness. At the root of the existing society there must be some great error which contradicted the natural order of things. By means of reason man could discover truth, defined as that which was consistent with nature. It was perfectly possible to organize society on a natural, as opposed to an artificial basis, and thereby ensure happiness for everyone. But if this was so feasible, why had it not been done? Because, said Owen, men have hitherto not been fully rational. They have not realized the extent to which their ideas, their actions, their whole characters have been conditioned by their environment. The beginning of wisdom is to be aware that "the character of man is formed for and not by him." Once the full significance of this is grasped it becomes possible to see truth instead of error, to act as a fully rational being. The springs of human behavior can now be understood, a "science of society" for the first time becomes possible, and the means of controlling human destiny is within men's grasp.

Thus far Owenism was within the bounds of the tradition of deism, reason, nature, associationism, and the ethics of enlightened (social) hedonism, stretching from David Hume and Adam Ferguson to Dugald Stewart. But at this point a new element entered into the Owenite calculation—the Industrial Revolution. The second major factor in Owenite thought was the social result and economic potential of industrialism. Underpinning Robert Owen's whole position was his success as a leader in the cotton industry, which was the pacemaker of the world's first industrial revolution. He was listened to with respect because of his success as a master cotton spinner, and he justified his social theories by appeal to his experience as a practical man of business. He made his mark in both of the two great centers of the new industry, Manchester and Glasgow.

It was in his early appreciation of the significance of the potentiality of material abundance that Owen was most ahead of other social reformers. Whatever the practical outcome of Owenite schemes, in theory Owenism was never backward-looking nor nostalgic. The vast increase in industrial productive capacity between 1790 and 1815 made possible an abundance hitherto undreamed of, argued Owen; and this would provide the necessary base for the good environment which would be productive of happy human beings. Happiness was, for the first time in human history, within the reach of all men. Only the contemporary system of society prevented the realization of this universal spread of the basis for happiness. Malthusian fears were groundless, since economic growth would take care of any conceivable increase in population. The production of wealth was sufficient to ensure happiness for all; poverty—and consequent denial of happiness—was caused by a wrong distribution of that wealth.

The phrenologists agreed that Owen's bump of benevolence was unusually large. Visitors to New Lanark, impressed by the mills and disarmed by Owen's charm, praised his practical benevolence and enlightened philanthropy. To a whole generation after 1815 he was "Mr. Owen, the Philanthropist," or "the benevolent Mr. Owen." His name was everywhere linked with successful, paternalistic schemes for improving the lot of the poor. Philanthropy was a basic motif in the pattern of Owenism.

Owen's plan for the reorganization of society (soon for the salvation of the world) originated as a scheme for relief of the unemployed. His philanthropic endeavors had first been directed to improving working and living conditions at New Lanark, then to educational reform and the restriction of child labor in factories. The "distress" which followed the peace of 1815 turned his attention to problems of the unemployed, and in this context he first elaborated his plan for self-supporting communities of about twelve hundred persons, with accommodation arranged in a parallelogram of buildings, and with provision for all the educational and social needs of the inhabitants. By 1820 these arrangements had matured into a communitarian plan for the thorough organization of society, embedded in a theory of cooperative socialism and prophetic utterance. But in the first instance Owenism developed within the dimensions of the Poor Laws as inherited from the late eighteenth century and aggravated by the impact of the Napoleonic Wars. It was no accident that the first Owenite organization in 1822 was named the British and Foreign Philanthropic Society for the Permanent Relief of the Labouring Classes, nor that philanthropists were conspicuous among Owen's early followers. In Britain the Owenite philanthropists included Scottish squires like Archibald James Hamilton, Irish landlords like William Thompson, and London businessmen such as John Minter Morgan. They were attracted to Owenism as a solution to the problems of poor relief, and after they had widened their horizons they still regarded it as an exercise in gentlemanly philanthropy. Their ideas of community were for the most part set in an agricultural mold and they strongly resented the values of industrialism.

In America Owenite philanthropy assumed a somewhat different hue. The Poor Law problem in its English form did not exist in the United States, nor was squirearchical paternalism appreciated except in parts of the

South. American philanthropy stemmed from other roots, usually either evangelical or radical, and this was reflected in the type of philanthropic support which American Owenism attracted. Thus on the one hand was Jeremiah Thompson, a wealthy Quaker merchant and shipowner of New York, who supported both New Harmony and Nashoba; on the other was William Maclure, philanthropic radical and deist. What there was not room for in the American environment was Owen's type of paternalism; as Maclure sagely observed: "The materials in this country are not the same as the cotton spinners at New Lanark, nor does the advice of a patron go so far."[21] The careers and interests of Owen and Maclure were very similar, and their ultimate disagreement after an initially enthusiastic collaboration may be explained as well by differences in the role of philanthropist in Britain and America as by differences in personality or educational policy.

It was not, however, as a scheme of philanthropy but as a plan for social reform that Owenism attracted its widest support. Owen and his followers have gone down in history as the main English school of utopian socialists, predecessors, together with their French contemporaries, the Saint-Simonians and Fourierists, of Marx and Engels. But the Owenites rejected the term utopian, and their socialism cannot be analyzed by the canons considered appropriate after the rise of modern socialism in the 1880's. Owenite socialism was (in the words of the *Cooperative Magazine* in 1827) "the true social or cooperative and communional system," a blend of communitarian theory, anticapitalist economics, and a science of society. These three elements made up the main part of

[21] Letter, Maclure to Mme. Fretageot, September 25, 1826. Bestor, *Education and Reform at New Harmony*, p. 371.

the doctrines of Owenism and together gave it distinctive characteristics as a philosophy of social reform. They also show the similarities and differences between American and British Owenism.

When Owenites spoke of their "communional system" they had several ideas in mind. In the first place they were referring to a general concept of community which they felt was essential for satisfactory human relationships in any society. The absence of such community was diagnosed by Owen as the chief ill of British society in the period 1814–1819: society was fragmented and turned against itself. In his efforts to restore harmony to society Owen became a socialist and was led to condemn all institutions which "individualized" man. Second, the communional system for many Owenites meant the holding of property in common and the abolition of individual ownership. Owen's position on this issue was not completely consistent, nor did he maintain the same views at different periods in his career. His followers similarly advocated varying degrees of communism, some wanting complete equality and community of goods, others content with a less absolute scheme. Third, there was an active belief in communitarianism as a method of social reform. Society was to be radically transformed by means of experimental communities, and this was regarded as a valid alternative to other methods of effecting societal change, such as revolution or legislation. In Britain and America there were traditions of community upon which the Owenites could draw in support of these three aspects of their communional system.

In Britain the communitarian element of Owenism had several roots. A paternalist rural tradition provided a favorable seeding ground for Owenite community ideas as a solution to agricultural distress and problems of improved husbandry. The Tory belief in an Old England which was a genuine community accounts for the presence of members of the squirearchy among Owenite apologists. Another aspect of community, stemming not from the Tories but from middle-class industrialists, was also associated with Owenism. This was the idea of community as an instrument of industrial relations. Early factory owners were faced with acute problems of labor shortage and labor discipline, and community provided a solution to some of these difficulties. Owen claimed that the germ of his communitarianism was in his experiences at New Lanark, the model factory village which his father-in-law, David Dale, had created to overcome problems of this sort. A third view of community was provided by an indigenous working-class culture of collectivism. In the later eighteenth century a network of friendly societies, burial clubs, and trade societies attested the strength of this "ethos of mutuality." Methodism reinforced it with the language of brotherhood and the essentially neighborhood institution of the chapel. The sense of the loss of community was expressed by contemporaries from Thomas Carlyle to Karl Marx. Owenites saw their task as the restoration of community values in a world which they described as artificial and atomized. Harmony was the keynote of the New Moral World, in sharp contrast with the discord of existing society. Neither the Owenites nor their contemporaries were able to define the problem of community in psychological terms, but they realized that the implications of industrialism could not be confined to physical changes. Owenism took account of the uniqueness of industrial society and sought to explain what industrialism was doing to the lives of ordinary people by reference to the concept of community.

In America there were other soils in which communitarianism could grow, notably religious sectarianism, and from this tradition the Owenites profited in several ways. Many of the millennial sects were also communitarian,[22] and with two of them—the Shakers and the Rappites—Owen and his followers were particularly familiar. Owen was interested in the Shakers long before he came to America;[23] and a few days after his first arrival here in November 1824 he visited the Shaker community at Niskeyuna, New York, and was much impressed. He had known of the Rappites at least since 1815. In 1820 he corresponded with Father Rapp about his community experiments, and in 1825 bought the settlement of Harmony, Indiana, from the Rappites for his own communitarian experiment of New Harmony. Owenism in America was thus physically and intellectually the inheritor of an established communitarian tradition, a secular version of sectarian communism.

There was a time when American communitarianism was explained in terms of the frontier, and Owenism, with its center in a pioneer settlement on the banks of the Wabash, fitted neatly into this pattern. But Bestor has argued convincingly that the frontier theory by itself is inadequate as an explanation.[24] Communitarianism did not originate on the frontier, nor were frontier conditions particularly favorable to its development. The

[22] For example, the Ephrata community, the Moravian Brethren, the Separatists of Zoar, Jemima Wilkinson's New Jerusalem, and the Mormons.

[23] In 1818 he published *A Brief Sketch of the Religious Society of People called Shakers* by W. S. Warder, a Philadelphia Quaker, and later received accounts of the Western Shakers and the Rappites from George Courtauld of Edinburgh.

[24] Arthur Eugene Bestor, "Patent-Office Models of the Good Society: Some Relationships between Social Reform and Westward Expansion," in *American Historical Review*, LVIII (1953), 505–526.

relationship between the growth of communitarianism and the rapid advance of the frontier in the first half of the nineteenth century is to be found in the more general concept of the West as it appeared to contemporaries. Communitarianism was a method of effecting social change by means of experimental communities and as such was in harmony with certain basic assumptions which Americans made about the West. In a period of rapid growth and unbounded confidence in the future, it was possible to believe that small experiments, if successful, could vitally affect the new society which was emerging—and it was urgent to seize this opportunity before it was too late. Older and more stable societies did not present this opportunity, but the West could be shaped by the conscious efforts of the present generation. Just as in Britain there was a widespread feeling among reformers until the 1830's that the changes wrought by industrial capitalism were not permanent, and it was therefore not too late to be able to build society on alternative principles, so in America there was an even stronger conviction that society in the West was in a state of flux, and that it was possible to fashion new institutions which would ensure a better world for the future. Owenite communitarianism was acceptable because it shared these assumptions about the nature of social change. And conversely, when it was clear that industrial capitalism in Britain and the institutions of individualism in America were so strongly established that they could not be radically affected by small-scale experiments, Owenism lost its rationale.

To Owenites as to other social reformers America seemed to be the ideal place for community experiments. Not only was land cheap and plentiful, but the intellectual climate was believed to be more favorable to social experiment. Owenites had little difficulty in discovering in the New World ideas and attitudes which were highly compatible with the new view of society. The origin of many aspects of Owenism lies in those elements of Enlightenment thought which were also influential in the early years of the Republic, so that a common base for sympathy and understanding was provided. Take, for instance, the case of agrarianism. In the late eighteenth and early nineteenth centuries radical movements were frequently agrarian, reflecting a concern with land and property reform in preindustrial societies. The Spencean Philanthropists were the main exponents of this philosophy in Britain and the similarity between Spenceanism and Owenism struck contemporaries. This agrarian bias in Owenism (which at first seems hard to reconcile with the image of Owen as one of the great success stories of the Industrial Revolution) harmonized well with the parallel development of the agrarian myth in America.[25] Within Owenism there was a strong strain of pastoralism, derived largely from eighteenth-century sources, and forming a common bond with other agrarians in America and Britain.[26]

The community element in Owenism thus had several different roots and references. Community in Britain and America was a recognizable concept, sufficiently familiar to be acceptable as a possible solution to a number of different social and economic problems—rural distress, labor shortage, feelings of alienation. Concepts of com-

[25] See Leo Marx, *The Machine in the Garden* (New York, 1964); Henry Nash Smith, *Virgin Land* (Cambridge, Mass., 1950; repr., New York, 1957), Book 3; Richard Hofstadter, *Age of Reform* (New York, 1956), Chap. 1.

[26] Pictorial evidence of this is provided in the illustrations of Owenite communities. A particularly fine example was published in John Minter Morgan, *Hampden in the Nineteenth Century*, 2 vols. (London, 1834).

munity in the two countries were similar in those aspects which stemmed from Enlightenment thought or from the problems of early industrialism. But there were differences when community ideas had other origins: for instance, religious sectarianism contained a much stronger bent toward community in America than in Britain, and the paternalistic community feeling of the English squirearchy was not indigenous in America. Owenism was able to draw on these different traditions impartially—hence the heterogeneous nature of the Owenite body. The Americans accepted Owen's (largely British) ideas of villages of cooperation, and the British Owenites waxed enthusiastic over American sectarian communities, especially the Shakers. Perhaps because of the greater strength of the communitarian tradition in America, Owenism was faced with stronger rivalry than in Britain. Thus, in the communitarian revival of the 1840's, Owenism in America was eclipsed by Fourierism, whereas in Britain Owenism remained the dominant communitarian doctrine, despite the attempted introduction of Fourierism and Saint-Simonism. That Owenism should have had a similar following in two such different societies as the British and American is partly explicable by the nature of its communitarian element. Ignoring political action and minimizing economic problems, communitarians concentrated on social and psychological questions; this provided a sufficient bond between reformers who, on both sides of the Atlantic, were in revolt against the dominant orthodoxies of their respective societies. For Americans, Owenism offered communitarianism without the trappings of religious sectarianism; in Britain, Owenite concepts of community provided a remedy for some of the tensions, social and personal, arising from early industrialism.

One further strand, interwoven with the foregoing,

completes the broad framework of Owenism. In the summer of 1817 Owen proclaimed the commencement of the millennium, and from then on the millennial note was present in most of his writings and also in the writings of some of his followers. It would be tedious to catalogue Owen's successive millennial announcements. His editorial in the first number of the *New Moral World* (November 1, 1834) was representative of innumerable statements both before and later:

The rubicon between the Old Immoral and the New Moral Worlds is finally passed: . . . This . . . is the great Advent of the world, the second coming of Christ,—for Truth and Christ are one and the same. The first coming of Christ was a parital development of Truth to the few. . . . The second coming of Christ will make Truth known to the many. . . . The time is therefore arrived when the foretold millennium is about to commence. . . .

Enthusiastic followers at New Harmony, and later at Harmony Hall, Queenwood, adopted a new chronology, dating their letters from the beginning of the new dispensation. At Harmony Hall the letters "C.M." (Commencement of the Millennium) were carved on the outside of the building. The social missionaries frequently played on the millennial theme. In the *New Moral World* and other Owenite journals many aspects of the culture of millennialism appeared. Contributors discussed biblical prophecy, the restoration of the Jews in relation to socialism, and animal magnetism as a herald of the millennium. Versifiers sent in millennial poems. Owenite converts wrote letters saying how much they longed for the day of salvation.

In extent and variety these millennial elements in Owenism conformed to certain recognizable variants within the general pattern of eighteenth- and nineteenth-century millennialism. Generally Owenites were inclined to be post- rather than premillennialists, although at times their precise position was confused. Owen was basically a typical eighteenth-century postmillennialist, believing that the millennium was simply a more perfect state of society, which could with equal propriety be called "the Rational State of Human Existence," or "The Brotherhood of the Human Race." But at times he spoke of a second advent and sudden cataclysm which implied a premillennialist position at variance with his previous meliorist statements. The interpretation of the millennium which was most favored by Owenites, including Owen himself, was inherited from those eighteenth-century millennialists who had secularized the idea of the millennium into a theory of evolutionary progress, by disguising Providence as natural law, and making reason and revelation embrace each other. The New Jerusalem became a state of universal happiness, the millennium a gradual progress toward human betterment. Such millennialists formed (in Professor Tuveson's words) "a bridge between the chiliasm of the seventeenth century and the liberal political progressivism of the nineteenth."[27] The Owenites helped to extend this bridge, and to carry farther, in popular (often crude) form, the secularization of the millennium.

Just why the Owenite movement should have adopted the form and rhetoric of a millenarian sect has perplexed and embarrassed most British writers. The existence of a continuing tradition of millennialism in America has long been recognized, and it is possible to document a two-way process of exchange between American Shakers, Swedenborgians, and Universalists on

[27] Ernest Lee Tuveson, *Millennium and Utopia* (Berkeley and Los Angeles, 1949), Harper Torchbook ed., p. 140.

the one hand and Owenite communitarians on the other. But an examination of evangelical religion in Britain and America suggests further clues. Owenism originated and flourished entirely within the grand era of evangelical ascendancy, *circa* 1800–1860. The central importance of evangelicalism, especially revivalism, in shaping the American mind in the nineteenth century has frequently been noted. But in Britain also, where a traditional religious establishment was more strongly entrenched, the same forces were at work for the spread of evangelical Christianity. One aspect of the evangelical heritage was particularly attractive to social reformers: in the biblical doctrine of the millennium they found a conceptual basis and a rhetoric for their ideas of utopia. The Owenites, like all social reformers, were faced with a problem of communication, how to ensure that their views could be made comprehensible to people who were still thinking along orthodox lines. The sect and the school became the models for effecting the new moral world. Owenism did not (as previous historians have suggested) "degenerate" into a "mere" sect after 1835, the implication being presumably that in its earlier stages it might have been something different, such as a political party or a mass movement of the working class. In fact, Owenism developed as a millennial and educational sect, not through failure to achieve some other institutional form, but through the logic of its need to communicate.

The new view of society which came out of this background of Scottish moral philosophy, Poor Law problems, philanthropy, communitarianism, and millennialism was presented in terms which, in their special combination, gave to Owenism a distinctive flavor. The struggle of Truth against Error, of Good against Evil, of Knowledge and Happiness against Ignorance, Misery, and Vice, was the language of Owenite controversy and propaganda. There was a constant harping on the search for consistency, for "where there is inconsistency there must be error," warned Owen.[28] The contrast between "artificial" and "natural" society was another frequent theme of Owenites. They were plagued by necessitarian controversies, and devoted a great deal of time to arguments about free will and human responsibility. Failure to convince opponents or to elicit adequate support for Owenite schemes was always attributed to the strength of prevailing prejudice, with its base in ignorance. Yet Owen remained confident of the final triumph, since reason and truth, "the principles on which this knowledge is founded, must ultimately and universally prevail."[29] Although a labor theory of value and anticapitalist economics were developed by some Owenites, notably William Thompson and John Gray, the general tone of Owenism was not economic, but social and moral. Its object was to establish the new moral world.

THE STEAM ENGINE OF THE MORAL WORLD

Few social reformers have accorded education such a central place in their philosophy as the Owenites. They spoke in lyrical terms of what could be achieved by it, and attributed vast power to its influence. Speaking at a dinner in Glasgow in 1812 in honor of the educationist, Joseph Lancaster, Owen declared:

By education . . . I now mean the instruction of all kinds which we receive from our earliest infancy until our characters are generally fixed and established . . . : it will be found to

[28] *Report to the County of Lanark*, in Owen, *Life*, IA, 281.
[29] *A New View of Society*, in Owen, *Life*, I, 300.

be . . . the primary source of all good and evil, misery and happiness which exist in the world . . . .[30]

The school and the lecture hall were prominent in all Owenite institutional arrangements. At new Lanark (the Mother Church of Owenism) the infant schools and the Institution for the Formation of Character attracted the most enthusiastic encomiums from the scores of visitors. The Edinburgh Practical Society,[31] the Orbiston community,[32] and New Harmony[33] conducted schools on advanced (usually Pestalozzian) lines. At New Harmony, William Maclure's efforts made the settlement a cultural and scientific center in the West which continued long after the communitarian efforts were ended. The various endeavors of the Cooperative and Economical Society of London,[34] and later of the British Association for Pro-

[30] *Glasgow Herald*, April 20, 1812; and Owen, *Life*, I, 249.

[31] The Practical Society of Edinburgh was an attempt to run an Owenite society in the years 1821-22. Its founder was Abram Combe. The membership was said to be from five to six hundred "heads of families," mostly mechanics and laborers. A day school with 128 children was established. See Donald Macdonald's account in the *New Harmony Gazette*, I (1826), 173-174; and obituary of Abram Combe in the *Orbiston Register*, September 19, 1827, pp. 65-71.

[32] Orbiston was the first British community to be organized and was on the Hamilton estate, about nine miles from Glasgow. The plan was begun in 1825 by Abram Combe and A. J. Hamilton, and came to an end after the death of Combe in 1827. The fullest account is in Alex. Cullen, *Adventures in Socialism* (Glasgow and London, 1910); but see also W. H. G. Armytage, *Heavens Below: Utopian Experiments in England, 1560-1960* (London and Toronto, 1961), pp. 96-104.

[33] The account of New Harmony in Bestor, *Backwoods Utopias*, Chap. 7, largely supersedes previous treatments of the subject.

[34] The London Cooperative and Economical Society was a working-class organization to promote Owenism, established in 1821 by a group of printers. A cooperative housing experiment at Spa Fields and a cooperative store were established. The goal was to set up a community but this was not attained. The main source of informa-

moting Cooperative Knowledge,[35] included lectures and discussions for the members and schools for their children. In all later Owenite ventures the same pattern of educational provision and priority was evident. Other contemporary bodies of reformers in Britain and America —the Working Men's Parties, the phrenologists, the Fourierists, the Chartists—had educational goals and used educational methods. But none was so continuously saturated with education as the Owenites. Their concern was not that of radical reformers who turned to "moral force" when "physical force" methods proved impracticable or inexpedient. They were committed to educational solutions from the very nature of their approach to problems of man and society. At times education (in Owen's sense of producing "the whole man") became for the Owenites not a means but the end itself. This primacy of concern for education was produced by the interacting and reinforcing nature of the various constituents of Owenism. Each constituent part, such as philanthropy, communitarianism, poor law, had an educational reference; and the interlocking of these constituents therefore produced in Owenism a powerful predilection for education.

As with all Owenite argument, the starting point for the discussion of education was happiness. Robert Dale

---

tion about the Society is Mudie's *Economist* (1821–22). See also Armytage, *Heavens Below*, pp. 92–95.

[35] The British Association for Promoting Cooperative Knowledge was formed in 1829 by a group of working-class radicals in London, with the aim of adapting Owen's basic ideas to working-class needs. It was mainly concerned with the promotion of cooperative stores. With the development of the agitation for parliamentary reform in 1831 its leading members became absorbed into the National Union of the Working Classes. See the *Cooperative Magazine* (1826–30), and William Lovett, *Life and Struggles* (London, 1876).

Owen, in his *Outline of the System of Education at New Lanark* (1824), assumed happiness as "our being's end and aim"; and went on: "Whatever . . . increases the happiness of the community is right; and whatever . . . tends to diminish that happiness is wrong." The individual's happiness is dependent on that of the community. Moreover, every action will be followed by its natural reward or punishment, that is, "the necessary consequences, immediate and remote, which result from any action." Education is concerned to bring knowledge and distinct conviction of the necessary consequences of conduct. This will be sufficient to direct the child; all rewards and punishments, except those of nature, are to be excluded. For nature has provided her own sanctions, and the child will therefore learn that nature's rewards will bring pleasure and her punishments, pain. The child's notion of right and wrong will be derived from the natural consequences of his conduct, not from artificial rewards and punishments: and the teacher will also strive to show him the intimate connection between his own happiness and that of others.

However philosophically incomplete this argument was (and it suffered from the difficulties inherent in all theories of hedonism or utilitarianism), it produced in the New Lanark and other Owenite schools a type of education greatly superior to the mechanical instruction of the age. A fundamental rule of kindness, not severity, to children was observed, and all harshness, anger, and violence were eschewed. A child who did wrong was to be pitied, not blamed, since he had not yet learned his own best self-interest. The material of instruction was chosen for its ability to hold the child's interest and adapted to his capacities. Visual aids, play methods, dancing, and singing were introduced, and the general emphasis was placed on child activity and participation. In the new schools the children were not to be taught by "the present defective and tiresome system of book learning" but by new methods of instruction "founded in nature."[36]

Most writers on Owen have remarked how the crucial role of education in his thought follows from his doctrine of character formation; and his stress on the importance of environment has prompted speculative comparisons with Locke and Helvetius. At the Lancaster dinner in 1812 Owen made his first public statement that ". . . we can materially command those circumstances which influence character"; and it is clear from the context that he was thinking of the effects of education on a community. Likewise, the famous passage in the first essay of *A New View of Society* referred to the influence of environment on a community:

Any general character, from the best to the worst, from the most ignorant to the most enlightened, may be given to any community, even to the world at large, by the application of proper means; which means are to a great extent at the command and under the control of those who have influence in the affairs of men.

Many contemporary liberal reformers and educationists were in broad agreement with this. It was when Owen developed his theory of individual character formation that he encountered most opposition and failed to secure the agreement of otherwise convinced Owenites. The fullest statement of his psychological views is in the *Book of the New Moral World* (1836), where he attempts to strike a mean between the influence of heredity and

[36] *Report to the County of Lanark*, in Owen, *Life*, IA, 297. See also the rules for an infant school laid down in ten points by Owen in his *Life*, I, 232-233, reprinted on pp. 173-175 below.

environment. Man is subject to the influence of his constitution at birth and to the influence of his external circumstances: but it was the latter element which Owen stressed as being the more important—perhaps because it was more obviously controllable. He hesitated to claim outright that inherited qualities ("constitution or organization at birth") could be altered by environment, although at times he apparently suggests this. It would seem that by heredity he was thinking not in biological but in social terms, and was thus emphasizing the importance of the social and cultural inheritance. Owenites consciously tried to think in social (as opposed to prevailing "individual, selfish") dimensions, and most of their arguments related to improvement by environment to the community, rather than to the individual in the first instance. The roots of this social psychology were in the moral philosophy of the Scottish Enlightenment, and can be traced similarly in James Mill and Dugald Stewart.[37] Owen did not accept fully the doctrine of associationism although his followers quoted passages from Dugald Stewart in support of their argument. In any case, belief in the effects of environment led to much the same position, especially in regard to the role of education.

From the premise of happiness, and through the doctrine of circumstances, the Owenites were led into educational paths, and other constituents of Owenism strengthened the trend in this direction. The Poor Law context of much early Owenite thought united ideas of unemployment relief, communitarianism, and philanthropy with education. "It is obvious," wrote Owen,

[37] See James Mill, *The Article "Education" reprinted from the Supplement to the Encyclopedia Britannica* (London, 1824); and Dugald Stewart, *Elements of the Philosophy of the Human Mind* (1792–1827), in *Collected Works*, edited by Sir William Hamilton, 11 vols. (Edinburgh, 1854–1860).

that training and education must be viewed as intimately connected with the employments of the association [i.e., community or "village of cooperation"]. The latter, indeed, will form an essential part of education under these arrangements. Each association, generally speaking, should create for itself a full supply of the usual necessaries, conveniences, and comforts of life.[38]

One of the fundamentals of Owenite social reform was that it provided radical change without violence or upheaval. "For some time to come," declared Owen,

there can be but one practicable, and therefore one rational reform which without danger can be attempted in these realms; a reform in which all men and all parties may join— that is, a reform in the training and in the management of the poor, the ignorant, the untaught and untrained, or ill-taught and ill-trained, among the whole mass of British population; and a plain, simple, practicable plan which would not contain the least danger to any individual or to any part of society, may be devised for the purpose.[39]

Education was to be the lever, first for dealing with the problem of the poor, but soon for effecting change throughout the whole of society.

It was of the essence of Owen's plan that the villages of cooperation should be self-supporting, and to link this principle with education was in harmony with strong contemporary predilections. The school of industry was the institutional result of this linkage and found much favor with Owenites. They were impressed with Fellenberg's school of industry at Hofwyl in Switzerland, and George Mudie typically devoted one issue of his paper, the *Economist* (March 24, 1821), to descriptions of Hofwyl and New Lanark. He quoted the object of Fellenberg in his school of industry as being

[38] *Report to the County of Lanark*, in Owen, *Life*, IA, 297.
[39] *A New View of Society*, in Owen, *Life*, I, 285.

to make the very employment of children, which is so essential to their subsistence, the means of their education, and thus to afford a solution of that most interesting problem, which seeks how to develop the moral and intellectual faculties, upon the most useful system, without taking one day from necessary manual labour.

William Maclure likewise favored industrial schools, partly because they were self-supporting, but also because they gave a "utilitarian" rather than an "ornamental" education. He admired Fellenberg's project of combining teaching on Pestalozzian principles with manual labor, which he considered especially suitable in America, where land was cheap and labor dear. The Americans ought to have been

the first people to put in practice so useful and necessary a procedure for the success, security and durability of our free and independent political association, that can only have a solid foundation on the knowledge of the great mass of productive labourers, who have the control of our government by universal suffrage.[40]

This was written in 1828; and in 1835 plans for a Manual Labor College at New Harmony were developed in detail. The idea of the school of industry had traveled far: first from its charity school origins in the seventeenth and early eighteenth centuries to the Society for Bettering the Conditions of the Poor in the 1790's; and thence to Owenite community education and the education for democracy in the New World.

In their communities the Owenites found yet further confirmation of the primary role of education. This process was two-sided. From the one side, progressive educationists had arrived at a concept of community as

---

[40] William Maclure, *Opinions on Various Subjects*, 3 vols. (New Harmony, Ind., 1831–38), I, 89.

integral to the educative process, and from the other, communitarians had come to regard education as their indispensable ally in building a successful community. In an over-all sense the experiment of community living was educational in that it aimed at rapidly diffusing "the dispositions, manners and mind" necessary for the success of the "new system." By this means, Owen told the communitarians at New Harmony, "a whole community can become a new people, have their minds born again, and be regenerated from the errors and corruptions which . . . have hitherto everywhere prevailed."[41] More specifically, he planned lectures three times a week for adult members of the community, convinced that if they were "well informed" they would not fail to be better (happier) communitarians. He was concerned to promote happy personal living among them, and was upset by their quarrels and grumblings and dishonesties. Only when they were brought to realize that anger and irritation were irrational, and that other men were not blameworthy, because their opinions were formed for them by environment, would the members of the community act and think charitably. At times the Owenites virtually despaired of the present generation, whose pernicious, antisocial habits had been formed so deeply by the old immoral system of society, and pinned all their hopes on the children. As a writer in the *New Harmony Gazette* (October 29, 1825) put it, "It is on the education of youth, the projector of the new social system relies for ultimate success."

There were other reasons, too, for the reinforcing relationship between communitarianism and education. William Thompson pointed out that it would be vain to teach children to love and respect one another if

[41] *New Harmony Gazette*, I (1826), 383.

they were "surrounded by the hourly example of all the bad passions that afflict humanity and give the lie to the good principles inculcated at school."[42] The community was regarded by Owenites as a social experiment, in which everything would be on record: "the whole of the arrangements form one grand moral as well as economical experiment."[43] There was here a great field of opportunity for the "enlightened moralist" to try out his social schemes, including educational plans. William Maclure was an admirer of Owen and was convinced of the soundness of his theory before coming to New Harmony. He sensed correctly that the atmosphere there would be congenial for the development of his educational interests, and he accordingly persuaded the Pestalozzian teachers, Mme. Fretageot, William Phiquepal, and Joseph Neef, to join the community. Maclure's scientific interests and his concern for the education of adults were similarly able to flourish in the New Harmony setting, despite his subsequent disillusionment with Owen.

For the Owenite who had not yet joined a community there was still a premium on education: this time it was as a preparation for community life. William Pare, addressing the members of the Birmingham Cooperative Society in 1828, warned his hearers that they should not think they understood the cooperative system perfectly; he therefore urged them to attend weekly meetings to hear lectures and discussions about it.[44]

Lastly, there was a deep Owenite faith in the pleasures

---

[42] Letter in *Cooperative Magazine,* III (1828), 43.
[43] William Thompson, *An Inquiry into the Principles of the Distribution of Wealth Most Conducive to Human Happiness* (London, 1824), p. 427.
[44] William Pare, *An Address Delivered at the Opening of the Birmingham Cooperative Society* (Birmingham, 1828), pp. 22–23.

of education.[45] At the back of most Owenite plans for community was a utopian vision of a propertyless, equalitarian society; of men working together in the fields, taking from the common stock according to their needs, and engaging in intellectual pursuits in their ample leisure time. In such a society there was neither luxury nor want. Work was a source of satisfaction and independence, and feelings of anger, envy, and all uncharitableness were dismissed as unworthy of a rational being. Into this picture fitted the concept of lifelong education. Schools, colleges, libraries, museums, scientific apparatus, lectures for adults—all appeared in profusion against a setting of arcadian bliss. It was easy to dismiss this vision as mere utopianism, but it had the practical function of sustaining the workers for the cause amid the disappointments and indifference of the old immoral world.

Thus from different angles the various aspects of Owenism came together, reaching a synthesis in educational terms. Education was a key for the Owenites because of their conviction that man's "ideas and habits . . . are the powers that govern and direct his conduct." And it followed that by education they meant not the "arts of reading and writing" but "the acquisition of ideas." "Education," wrote Abram Combe,

means the ideas which are impressed on the mind of the individual, by which his judgment is formed, and by which the bent is given, in a great measure, to his inclinations. The desire of respect or approbation appears to be the mainspring; and this spring, it will be found, may be made to pull in any direction.[46]

[45] See William Thompson, *Practical Directions for the Speedy and Economical Establishment of Communities* (London, 1830), pp. 205–225, "Education and Mental Pleasures."
[46] Abram Combe, *Metaphorical Sketches of the Old and New Systems* (Edinburgh, 1823), p. 99.

There was a breadth in the Owenite conception of education which was frightening to orthodox religious and social opinion of the early nineteenth century, and the reaction to it was therefore hostile and scornful. Perhaps Owen was correct when he diagnosed: "I am termed a visionary only because my principles have originated in experiences too comprehensive for the limited locality in which people have hitherto been interested."[47]

Not all the components of Owenism were found in equal measure in the intellectual make-up of any individual Owenite. His social, economic, and national status inclined him to emphasize some aspects and to neglect others. A background of eighteenth-century moral philosophy was probably the strongest common bond between British and American Owenites. The Poor Laws, paternalism, and industrialism contributed comparatively little to American Owenism, whereas the millennial and communitarian traditions were stronger than in Britain. Despite the differences between American and British society in the 1820's, the Owenites tended to think of an educational pattern common to both countries. A school run on the principles of Pestalozzi, Fellenberg, or Owen was sufficiently unusual to be detached from its contemporary surroundings, whether in America or Britain. And the importance which Owenites attributed to the informal educational influences of the social environment was equally applicable in either country. The primary role of education for the Owenite was to produce men and women suitable for a new moral world, which was not yet in existence. As the Owenite printer, George Mudie, said, the school was "the steam engine of the moral world."[48]

[47] See Owen, *Life,* IA, 102, 218.
[48] *Economist,* I (1826), 96.

SUGGESTIONS FOR FURTHER READING

A general interpretation and full bibliography is given in J. F. C. Harrison, *Quest for the New Moral World: Robert Owen and the Owenites in Britain and America* (London and New York, 1968), and the following list is therefore confined to books which are fairly easily available.

The best life of Owen is still Frank Podmore, *Robert Owen: A Biography*, 2 vols. (London and New York, 1906; a later ed., 1923), but it should be supplemented with G. D. H. Cole, *Life of Robert Owen*, 3rd ed. (New York, 1966), and Margaret Cole, *Robert Owen of New Lanark, 1771-1858* (New York, 1953). Rowland Hill Harvey, *Robert Owen: Social Idealist* (Berkeley and Los Angeles, 1949), does not add much to these.

The outstanding work on American communitarianism is Arthur Eugene Bestor, Jr., *Backwoods Utopias: The Sectarian and Owenite Phases of Communitarian Socialism in America, 1663-1829* (Philadelphia, 1950). Older works which are still very useful are Charles Nordhoff, *The Communistic Societies of the United States* (New York, 1875; repr., 1961); John Humphrey Noyes, *History of American Socialisms* (Philadelphia, 1870; repr., New York, 1961); and George B. Lockwood, *The New Harmony Movement* (New York, 1905). There is a large literature on New Harmony, but the two most recent works are William E. Wilson, *The Angel and the Serpent* (Bloomington, Ind., 1964), and Karl J. R. Arndt, *George Rapp's Harmony Society, 1785-1847* (Philadelphia, 1965). An important biography is R. W. Leopold, *Robert Dale Owen* (Cambridge, Mass., 1940). For British communitarianism, see W. H. G. Armytage, *Heavens Below: Utopian Experiments in England, 1560-1960*

(London and Toronto, 1961). A study of Owen and Owenite education in Britain is Harold Silver, *The Concept of Popular Education: A Study of Ideas and Social Movements in the Early Nineteenth Century* (London, 1965); and there are useful sections on Owenism in Brian Simon, *Studies in the History of Education, 1780–1870* (London, 1960), and W. A. C. Stewart and W. P. McCann, *The Educational Innovators, 1750–1880* (New York, 1967).

Copies of Owen's works are not too easy to find outside the larger university libraries and two selections are therefore welcome. The first, edited by G. D. H. Cole, is Owen, *A New View of Society and Other Writings* (Everyman's Library, London and New York, 1963), and includes Owen's chief writings up to 1820. The second is A. L. Morton, *The Life and Ideas of Robert Owen* (London, 1962). On Maclure, see Arthur Eugene Bestor, Jr., *Education and Reform at New Harmony: Correspondence of William Maclure and Marie Duclos Fretageot, 1820–1833* (Indianapolis, 1948). A valuable account of people in the British Owenite movement, written by an old Owenite, is George Jacob Holyoake, *History of Cooperation in England* (London, 1906).

1. Robert Owen: A New View of Society

In his first and most important work, A New View of Society *(London, 1813–1814), Owen set out his theory of character formation and described the social experiments at his factory-village of New Lanark in Scotland. He always regarded his achievements at New Lanark as the basis for his communitarian and educational plans. These extracts are reprints of the first two essays and part of the third from the* Life *of Robert Owen, Written by Himself.**

ESSAYS ON THE FORMATION OF CHARACTER

First Essay

Any general character, from the best to the worst, from the most ignorant to the most enlightened, may be given to any community, even to the world at large, by the application of proper means; which means are to a great extent at the command and under the control of those who have influence in the affairs of men.

According to the last returns under the Population Act, the poor and working classes of Great Britain and Ireland have been found to exceed fifteen millions of per-

* Two volumes, numbered I and IA (London, 1857–1858), I, 265–286, and 292–294.

sons, or nearly three-fourths of the population of the British Islands.

The characters of these persons are now permitted to be very generally formed without proper guidance or direction, and, in many cases, under circumstances which directly impel them to a course of extreme vice and misery; thus rendering them the worst and most dangerous subjects in the empire; while the far greater part of the remainder of the community are educated upon the most mistaken principles of human nature, such, indeed, as cannot fail to produce a general conduct throughout society, totally unworthy of the character of rational beings.

The first thus unhappily situated are the poor and the uneducated profligate among the working classes, who are now trained to commit crimes, for the commission of which they are afterwards punished.

The second is the remaining mass of the population, who are now instructed to believe, or at least to acknowledge, that certain principles are unerringly true, and to act as though they were grossly false; thus filling the world with folly and inconsistency, and making society, throughout all its ramifications, a scene of insincerity and counteraction.

In this state the world has continued to the present time; its evils have been and are continually increasing; they cry aloud for efficient corrective measures, which if we longer delay, general disorder must ensue.

"But," say those who have not deeply investigated the subject, "attempts to apply remedies have been often made, yet all of them have failed. The evil is now of a magnitude not to be controlled; the torrent is already too strong to be stemmed; and we can only wait with fear or calm resignation to see it carry destruction in its course, by confounding all distinctions of right and wrong."

Such is the language now held, and such are the general feelings on this most important subject.

These, however, if longer suffered to continue, must lead to the most lamentable consequences. Rather than pursue such a course, the character of legislators would be infinitely raised, if, forgetting the petty and humiliating contentions of sects and parties, they would thoroughly investigate the subject, and endeavour to arrest and overcome these mighty evils.

The chief object of these Essays is to assist and forward investigations of such vital importance to the well-being of this country, and of society in general.

The view of the subject which is about to be given has arisen from extensive experience for upwards of twenty years, during which period its truth and importance have been proved by multiplied experiments. That the writer may not be charged with precipitation or presumption, he has had the principle and its consequences, examined, scrutinised, and fully canvassed, by some of the most learned, intelligent, and competent characters of the present day: who, on every principle of duty as well as of interest, if they had discovered error in either, would have exposed it;—but who, on the contrary, have fairly acknowledged their incontrovertible truth and practical importance.

Assured, therefore, that his principles are true, he proceeds with confidence, and courts the most ample and free discussion of the subject; courts it for the sake of humanity—for the sake of his fellow creatures—millions of whom experience sufferings which, were they to be unfolded, would compel those who govern the world to exclaim—"Can these things exist and we have no knowledge of them?" But they do exist—and even the heart-rending statements which were made known to the public during the discussions upon negro-slavery, do not exhibit more afflicting scenes than those which, in various parts of the world, daily arise from the injustice of society towards itself; from the inattention of mankind to the circumstances which incessantly surround them; and from the want of a correct knowledge of human nature in those who govern and control the affairs of men.

If these circumstances did not exist to an extent almost incredible, it would be unnecessary now to contend for a principle regarding Man, which scarcely requires more than to be fairly stated to make it self-evident.

This principle is, that *"Any general character, from the best to the worst, from the most ignorant to the most enlightened, may be given to any community, even to the world at large, by the application of proper means; which means are to a great extent at the command and under the control of those who have influence in the affairs of men."*

The principle as now stated is a broad one, and, if it should be found to be true, cannot fail to give a new character to legislative proceedings, and such a character as will be most favourable to the well-being of society.

That this principle is true to the utmost limit of the terms, is evident from the experience of all past ages, and from every existing fact.

Shall misery, then, most complicated and extensive, be experienced, from the prince to the peasant, throughout all the nations of the world, and shall its cause and the means of its prevention be known, and yet these means withheld? The undertaking is replete with difficulties which can only be overcome by those who have influence in society: who, by foreseeing its important practical benefits, may be induced to contend against those difficulties; and who, when its advantages are clearly seen and strongly felt, will not suffer individual considerations to be put in competition with their attainment. It is true their ease and comfort may be for a time sacrificed to those prejudices; but, if they persevere, the principles on which this knowledge is founded must ultimately universally prevail.

In preparing the way for the introduction of these principles, it cannot now be necessary to enter into the detail of facts to prove that children can be trained to acquire *"any language, sentiments, belief, or any bodily habits and manners, not contrary to human nature."*

For that this has been done, the history of every nation of which we have records, abundantly confirms; and that this is, and may be again done, the facts which exist around us and throughout all the countries in the world, prove to demonstration.

Possessing, then, the knowledge of a power so important, which when understood, is capable of being wielded with the certainty of a law of nature, and which would gradually remove the evils which now chiefly afflict mankind, shall we permit it to remain dormant and useless, and suffer the plagues of society perpetually to exist and increase?

No: the time is now arrived when the public mind of this country, and the general state of the world, call imperatively for the introduction of this all-pervading principle, not only in theory, but into practice.

Nor can any human power now impede its rapid progress. Silence will not retard its course, and opposition will give increased celerity to its movements. The commencement of the work will, in fact, ensure its accomplishment; henceforth all the irritating angry passions, arising from ignorance of the true cause of bodily and mental character, will gradually subside, and be replaced by the most frank and conciliating confidence and good-will.

Nor will it be possible hereafter for comparatively a few individuals, unintentionally to occasion the rest of mankind to be surrounded by circumstances which inevitably form such characters as they afterwards deem it a duty and a right to punish even to death; and that, too, while they themselves have been the instruments of forming those characters. Such proceedings not only create innumerable evils to the directing few, but essentially retard them and the great mass of society from attaining the enjoyment of a high degree of positive happiness. Instead of punishing crimes after they have permitted the human character to be formed so as to commit them, they will adopt the only means which can be adopted to prevent the existence of those crimes; means by which they may be most easily prevented.

Happily for poor traduced and degraded human nature, the principle for which we now contend will speedily divest it of all the ridiculous and absurd mystery with which it has been hitherto enveloped by the ignorance of preceding times: and all the complicated and counteracting motives for good conduct, which have been multiplied almost to infinity, will be reduced to one single principle of action, which, by its evident operation and sufficiency, shall render this intricate system unnecessary, and ultimately supersede it in all parts of the earth. That principle is *the happiness of self, clearly understood and uniformly practised; which can only be attained by conduct that must promote the happiness of the community*.

For that Power which governs and pervades the universe has evidently so formed man, that he must progressively pass from a state of ignorance to intelligence, the limits of which it is not for man himself to define; and in that progress to discover, that his individual happiness can be increased and extended only in proportion as he actively endeavours to increase and extend the happiness of all around him. The principle admits neither of exclusion nor of limitation; and such appears evidently the state of the public mind, that it will now seize and cherish this principle as the most precious boon which it has yet been allowed to attain. The errors of all opposing motives will appear in their true light, and the ignorance whence they arose will become so glaring, that even the most unenlightened will speedily reject them.

For this state of matters, and for all the gradual changes contemplated, the extraordinary events of the present times have essentially contributed to prepare the way.

Even the late Ruler of France, although immediately influenced by the most mistaken principles of ambition, has contributed to this happy result, by shaking to its foundation that mass of superstition and bigotry, which on the continent of Europe had been accumulating for ages, until it had so overpowered and depressed the human intellect, that to attempt improvement without its removal would have been most unavailing. And in the next place, by carrying the mistaken selfish principles in which mankind have been hitherto educated to the extreme in practice, he has rendered their error manifest, and left no doubt of the fallacy of the source whence they originated.

These transactions, in which millions have been immolated, or consigned to poverty and bereft of friends, will be preserved in the records of time, and impress future ages with a just estimation of the principles now about to be introduced into practice; and will thus prove perpetually useful to all succeeding generations.

For the direful effects of Napoleon's government have created the most deep-rooted disgust at notions which could produce a belief that such conduct was glorious, or calculated to increase the happiness of even the individual by whom it was pursued.

And the late discoveries and proceedings of the Rev. Dr. Bell and Mr. Joseph Lancaster have also been preparing the way, in a manner the most opposite, but yet not less effectual, by directing the public attention to the beneficial effects, on the young and unresisting mind, of even the limited education which their systems embrace.

They have already effected enough to prove that all which is now in contemplation respecting the training of youth may be accomplished without fear of disappointment. And by so doing, as the consequences of their improvements cannot be confined within the British Isles, they will for ever be ranked among the most important benefactors of the human race. But henceforward to contend for any new exclusive system will be in vain: the public mind is already too well informed, and has too far passed the possibility of retrogression, much longer to permit the continuance of any such evil.

For it is now obvious that such a system must be destructive of the happiness of the excluded, by their seeing others enjoy what they are not permitted to possess; and also that it tends, by creating opposition from the justly injured feelings of the excluded, in proportion to the extent of the exclusion, to diminish the happiness even of the privileged: the former therefore can have no rational motive for its continuance.

A New View of Society

If, however, owing to the irrational principles by which the world has been hitherto governed, individuals, or sects, or parties, shall yet by their plans of exclusion attempt to retard the amelioration of society, and prevent the introduction into PRACTICE of that truly just spirit which knows no exclusion, such facts shall yet be brought forward as cannot fail to render all their efforts vain.

It will therefore be the essence of wisdom in the privileged class to co-operate sincerely and cordially with those who desire not to touch one iota of the supposed advantages which they now possess; and whose first and last wish is to increase the particular happiness of those classes, as well as the general happiness of society. A very little reflection on the part of the privileged will ensure this line of conduct; whence, without domestic revolution—without war or bloodshed—nay, without prematurely disturbing any thing which exists, the world will be prepared to receive principles which are alone calculated to build up a system of happiness, and to destroy those irritable feelings which have so long afflicted society,—solely because society has hitherto been ignorant of the true means by which the most useful and valuable character may be formed.

This ignorance being removed, experience will soon teach us how to form character, individually and generally, so as to give the greatest sum of happiness to the individual and to mankind.

These principles require only to be known in order to establish themselves; the outline of our future proceedings then becomes clear and defined, nor will they permit us henceforth to wander from the right path. They direct that the governing powers of all countries should establish rational plans for the education and general formation of the characters of their subjects. *These plans must be devised to train children from their earliest infancy in good habits of every description (which will of course prevent them from acquiring those of falsehood and deception). They must afterwards be rationally educated, and their labour be usefully directed. Such habits and education will impress them with an active and ardent desire to promote the happiness of every individual, and that without the* shadow of exception *for sect, or party, or country, or climate. They will also ensure, with the fewest possible exceptions, health, strength, and vigour of body; for the happiness of man can be erected only on the foundations of health of body and peace of mind.*

And that health of body and peace of mind may be preserved sound and entire, through youth and manhood, to old age, it becomes equally necessary that the irresistible propensities which form a part of his nature, and which now produce the endless and ever multiplying evils with which humanity is afflicted, should be so directed as to increase and not to counteract his happiness.

The knowledge however thus introduced will make it evident to the understanding, that by far the greater part of the misery with which man is encircled *may* be easily dissipated and removed; and that with mathematical precision he *may* be surrounded with those circumstances which must gradually increase his happiness.

Hereafter, when the public at large shall be satisfied that these principles *can* and *will* withstand the ordeal through which they must inevitably pass; when they shall prove themselves true to the clear comprehension and certain conviction of the unenlightened as well as the learned; and when, by the irresistible power of truth, detached from falsehood, they shall establish themselves in the mind, no more to be removed but by the entire annihilation of human intellect; then the consequent practice which they direct shall be explained, and rendered easy of adoption.

In the meantime, let no one anticipate evil, even in the slightest degree, from these principles; they are not innoxious only, but pregnant with consequences to be wished and desired beyond all others by *every* individual in society.

Some of the best intentioned among the various classes in society may still say, "All this is *very delightful and very beautiful in theory,* but *visionaries* alone expect to see it *realized."* To this remark only one reply *can* or *ought* to be made; that *these principles have been carried most successfully into practice.*

(The beneficial effects of this practice have been experienced for many years among a population of between two and three thousand at New Lanark, in Scotland; at Munich, in Bavaria; and in the Pauper Colonies, at Fredericks-oord.)

The present Essays, therefore, are not brought forward as mere matter of speculation, to amuse the idle visionary who *thinks* in his closet, and never *acts* in the world; but to create universal activity, pervade society with a knowledge of its true interests, and direct the public mind to the most important object to which it can be directed,—to a national proceeding for rationally forming the character of that immense mass of population which is now allowed to be so formed as to fill the world with crimes.

Shall questions of merely local and temporary interest, whose ultimate results are calculated only to withdraw pecuniary profits from one set of individuals and give them to others, engage day after day the attention of politicians and ministers; call forth petitions and delegates from the widely spread agricultural and commercial interests of the empire;—and shall the well-being of millions of the poor, half-naked, half-famished, untaught, and untrained, hourly increasing to a most alarming extent in these islands, not call forth *one* petition, *one* delegate, or *one* rational effective legislative measure?

No! for such has been our education, that we hesitate not to devote years and expend millions in the *detection* and *punishment* of crimes, and in the attainment of objects whose ultimate results are, in comparison with this, insignificancy itself: and yet we have not moved one step in the true path to *prevent* crimes, and to diminish the innumerable evils with which mankind are now afflicted.

Are these false principles of conduct in those who govern the world to influence mankind permanently? And if not, *how,* and *when* is the change to commence?

These important considerations shall form the subject of the next Essay.

Second Essay

The Principles of the Former Essay continued, and applied in part to Practice.

It is not unreasonable to hope that *hostility* may *cease,* even where *perfect agreement cannot be established.* If we cannot *reconcile all opinions,* let us endeavour to unite all hearts.— Mr. Vansittart's Letter to the Rev. Dr. Herbert Marsh.

General principles only were developed in the First Essay. In this an attempt will be made to show the advantages which may be derived from the adoption of those principles into practice, and to explain the mode by which the practice may, without inconvenience, be generally introduced.

Some of the most important benefits to be derived from the introduction of those principles into practice are, that they will create the most cogent reasons to induce each man "to have charity for *all* men." No feeling short of this can indeed find place in any mind which has been taught clearly to understand that children in all parts of the earth have been, are, and everlastingly will be, impressed with habits and sentiments similar to those of their parents and instructors; modified, however, by the cirumstances in which they have been, are, or may be placed, and by the peculiar organisation of each individual. Yet not one of these causes of character is at the command, or in any manner under the control, of infants, who (whatever absurdity we may have been taught to the contrary,) cannot possibly be accountable for the sentiments and manners which may be given to them. And here lies the fundamental error of society; and from hence have proceeded, and do proceed, most of the miseries of mankind.

Children are, without exception, passive and wonderfully contrived compounds; which, by an accurate previous and subsequent attention, *founded on a correct knowledge of the subject,* may be formed collectively to have any human character. And although these compounds, like all the other works of nature, possess endless varieties, yet they partake of that plastic quality, which, by perseverance under judicious management, may be ultimately moulded into the very image of rational wishes and desires.

In the next place these principles cannot fail to create

feelings which, without force or the production of any counteracting motive, will irresistibly lead those who possess them to make due allowance for the difference of sentiments and manners, not only among their friends and countrymen, but also among the inhabitants of every region of the earth, even including their enemies. With this insight into the formation of character, there is no conceivable foundation for private displeasure or public enmity. Say, if it be within the sphere of possibility that children can be trained to attain *that* knowledge, and at the same time to acquire feelings of enmity towards a single human creature? The child who from infancy has been rationally instructed in these principles, will readily discover and trace *whence* the opinions and habits of his associates have arisen, and *why* they possess them. At the same age he will have acquired reason sufficient to exhibit to him forcibly the irrationality of being angry with an individual for possessing qualities which, as a passive being during the formation of those qualities, he had not the means of preventing. Such are the impressions these principles will make on the mind of every child so taught; and, instead of generating anger or displeasure, they will produce commiseration and pity for those individuals who possess either habits or sentiments which appear to him to be destructive of their own comfort, pleasure, or happiness; and will produce on his part a desire to remove those causes of distress, that his own feelings of commiseration and pity may be also removed. The pleasure which he cannot avoid experiencing by this mode of conduct will likewise stimulate him to the most active endeavours to withdraw those circumstances which surround any part of mankind with causes of misery, and to replace them with others which have a tendency to increase happiness. He

A New View of Society

will then also strongly entertain the desire "to do good to *all* men," and even to those who think themselves his enemies.

Thus *shortly, directly,* and *certainly* may mankind be taught the essence, and to attain the ultimate object, of all former *moral* and *religious* instruction.

These Essays, however, are intended to explain that which is *true,* and not to attack that which is *false.* For to explain that which is true may permanently improve, without creating even temporary evil; whereas to attack that which is false, is often productive of very fatal consequences. The former convinces the judgment when the mind possesses full and deliberate powers of judging; the latter instantly arouses irritation, and renders the judgment unfit for its office, and useless. But why should we *ever* irritate? Do not these principles make it so obvious as to place it beyond any doubt, that even the present irrational ideas and practices prevalent throughout the world are not to be charged as either a fault or a culpable error of the existing generation? The immediate cause of them was the partial ignorance of our forefathers, who, although they acquired some vague disjointed knowledge of the principles on which character is formed, could not discover the connected chain of those principles, and consequently knew not how to apply them to practice. They taught their children that which they had themselves been taught, that which they had acquired, and in so doing they acted like their forefathers; who retained the established customs of former generations until better and superior were discovered and made evident to them.

The present race of men have also instructed their children as they had been previously instructed, and are equally unblameable for any defects which their systems contain. And however erroneous or injurious that instruction and those systems may now be proved to be, the principles on which these Essays are founded will be misunderstood, and their spirit will be wholly misconceived, if either irritation or the slightest degree of ill-will shall be generated against those who even tenaciously adhere to the worst parts of that instruction, and support the most pernicious of those systems. For such individuals, sects, or parties have been trained from infancy to consider it their duty and interest so to act, and in so acting they merely continue the customs of their predecessors. Let truth unaccompanied with error be placed before them; give them time to examine it and to see that it is in unison with all previously ascertained truths; and conviction and acknowledgment of it will follow of course. It is weakness itself to require assent *before* conviction; and *afterwards* it will not be withheld. To endeavour to force conclusions without making the subject clear to the understanding, is most unjustifiable and irrational, and must prove useless or injurious to the mental faculties.

In the spirit thus described we therefore proceed in the investigation of the subject.

The facts which by the invention of printing have gradually accumulated now show the errors of the systems of our forefathers so distinctly, that they must be, when pointed out, evident to all classes of the community, and render it absolutely necessary that new legislative measures be immediately adopted to prevent the confusion which must arise from even the most ignorant being competent to detect the absurdity and glaring injustice of many of those laws by which they are now governed.

Such are those laws which enact punishments for a

A New View of Society

very great variety of actions designated crimes; while those from whom such actions proceed are regularly trained to acquire no other knowledge than that which compels them to conclude that those actions are the best they could perform.

How much longer shall we continue to allow generation after generation to be taught crime from their infancy, and, when so taught, hunt them like beasts of the forest, until they are entangled beyond escape in the toils and nets of the law? when, if the circumstances of those poor unpitied sufferers had been reversed with those who are ever surrounded with the pomp and dignity of justice, these latter would have been at the bar of the culprit, and the former would have been in the judgment seat.

Had the present Judges of these realms been born and educated among the poor and profligate of St. Giles's or some similar situation, is it not certain, inasmuch as they possess native energies and abilities, that ere this they would have been at the head of their *then* profession, and, in consequence of that superiority and proficiency, would have already suffered imprisonment, transportation, or death? Can we for a moment hesitate to decide, that if some of those men whom the laws dispensed by the present Judges have doomed to suffer capital punishments, had been born, trained, and circumstanced, as these Judges were born, trained, and circumstanced, that some of those who had so suffered would have been the identical individuals who would have passed the same awful sentences on the present highly esteemed dignitaries of the law?

If we open our eyes and attentively notice events, we shall observe these facts to multiply before us. Is the evil then of so small magnitude as to be totally disregarded and passed by as the ordinary occurrences of the day, and as not deserving of one reflection? And shall we be longer told "that the convenient time to attend to inquiries of this nature is not yet come: that other matters of far weightier import engage our attention, and it must remain over till a season of more leisure?"

To those who may be inclined to think and speak thus, I would say—"Let feelings of humanity or strict justice induce you to devote a few hours to visit some of the public prisons of the metropolis, and patiently inquire, with kind commiserating solicitude, of their various inhabitants, the events of their lives and the lives of their various connections. They will tales unfold that *must* arrest attention, that will disclose sufferings, misery, and injustice, upon which, for obvious reasons, I will not now dwell, but which previously, I am persuaded, you could not suppose it possible to exist in any civilised state, far less that they should be permitted for centuries to increase around the very fountain of British jurisprudence." The true cause, however, of this conduct, so contrary to the general humanity of the natives of these Islands, is, that a practical remedy for the evil, on clearly defined and sound principles, had not yet been suggested. But the principles developed in this "New View of Society," *will point out a remedy which is almost simplicity itself, possessing no more practical difficulties than many of the common employments of life; and such as are readily overcome by men of very ordinary practical talents.*

That such a remedy is easily practicable, may be collected from the account of the following very partial experiment.

In the year 1784 the late Mr. Dale, of Glasgow, founded a manufactory for spinning of cotton, near the

A New View of Society

falls of the Clyde, in the county of Lanark, in Scotland; and about that period cotton mills were first introduced into the northern part of the kingdom.

It was the power which could be obtained from the falls of water that induced Mr. Dale to erect his mills in this situation; for in other respects it was not well chosen. The country around was uncultivated; the inhabitants were poor and few in number; and the roads in the neighbourhood were so bad, that the Falls, now so celebrated, were then unknown to strangers.

It was therefore necessary to collect a new population to supply the infant establishment with labourers. This, however, was no light task; for all the regularly trained Scotch peasantry disdained the idea of working early and late, day after day, within cotton mills. Two modes then only remained of obtaining these labourers; the one, to procure children from the various public charities of the country; and the other, to induce families to settle around the works.

To accommodate the first, a large house was erected, which ultimately contained about five hundred children, who were procured chiefly from workhouses and charities in Edinburgh. These children were to be fed, clothed, and educated; and these duties Mr. Dale performed with the unwearied benevolence which it is well known he possessed.

To obtain the second, a village was built; and the houses were let at a low rent to such families as could be induced to accept employment in the mills; but such was the general dislike to that occupation at the time, that, with a few exceptions, only persons destitute of friends, employment, and character, were found willing to try the experiment; and of these a sufficient number to supply a constant increase of the manufactory could not be obtained. It was therefore deemed a favour on the part even of such individuals to reside at the village, and, when taught the business, they grew so valuable to the establishment, that they became agents not to be governed contrary to their own inclinations.

Mr. Dale's principal avocations were at a distance from the works, which he seldom visited more than once for a few hours in three or four months; he was therefore under the necessity of committing the management of the establishment to various servants with more or less power.

Those who have a practical knowledge of mankind will readily anticipate the character which a population so collected and constituted would acquire. It is therefore scarcely necessary to state, that the community by degrees was formed under these circumstances into a very wretched society: every man did that which was right in his own eyes, and vice and immorality prevailed to a monstrous extent. The population lived in idleness, in poverty, in almost every kind of crime; consequently, in debt, out of health, and in misery. Yet to make matters still worse,—although the cause proceeded from the best possible motive, a conscientious adherence to principle,—the whole was under a strong sectarian influence, which gave a marked and decided preference to one set of religious opinions over all others, and the professors of the favoured opinions were the privileged of the community.

The boarding-house containing the children presented a very different scene. The benevolent proprietor spared no expense to give comfort to the poor children. The rooms provided for them were spacious, always clean, and well ventilated; the food was abundant, and of the best quality; the clothes were neat and useful; a surgeon

A New View of Society

was kept in constant pay, to direct how to prevent or cure disease; and the best instructors which the country afforded were appointed to teach such branches of education as were deemed likely to be useful to children in their situation. Kind and well-disposed persons were appointed to superintend all their proceedings. Nothing, in short, at first sight seemed wanting to render it a most complete charity.

But to defray the expense of these well devised arrangements, and to support the establishment generally, it was absolutely necessary that the children should be employed within the mills from six o'clock in the morning till seven in the evening, summer and winter; and after these hours their education commenced. The directors of the public charities, from mistaken economy, would not consent to send the children under their care to cotton mills, unless the children were received by the proprietors at the ages of six, seven, and eight. And Mr. Dale was under the necessity of accepting them at those ages, or of stopping the manufactory which he had commenced.

It is not to be supposed that children so young could remain, with the intervals of meals only, from six in the morning until seven in the evening, in constant employment, on their feet, within cotton mills, and afterwards acquire much proficiency in education. And so it proved; for many of them became dwarfs in body and mind, and some of them were deformed. Their labour through the day and their education at night became so irksome, that numbers of them continually ran away, and almost all looked forward with impatience and anxiety to the expiration of their apprenticeship of seven, eight, and nine years, which generally expired when they were from thirteen to fifteen years old. At this period of life, unaccustomed to provide for themselves, and unacquainted with the world, they usually went to Edinburgh or Glasgow, where boys and girls were soon assailed by the innumerable temptations which all large towns present, and to which many of them fell sacrifices.

Thus Mr. Dale's arrangements, and his kind solicitude for the comfort and happiness of these children, were rendered in their ultimate effect almost nugatory. They were hired by him and sent to be employed, and without their labour he could not support them; but, while under his care, he did all that any individual, circumstanced as he was, could do for his fellow-creatures. The error proceeded from the children being sent from the workhouses at an age much too young for employment. They ought to have been detained four years longer, and educated; and then some of the evils which followed would have been prevented.

If such be a true picture, not overcharged, of parish apprentices to our manufacturing system, under the best and most humane regulations, in what colours must it be exhibited under the worst?

Mr. Dale was advancing in years: he had no son to succeed him; and, finding the consequences just described to be the result of all his strenuous exertions for the improvement and happiness of his fellow-creatures, it is not surprising that he became disposed to retire from the cares of the establishment. He accordingly sold it to some English merchants and manufacturers; one of whom, under the circumstances just narrated, undertook the management of the concern, and fixed his residence in the midst of the population. This individual had been previously in the management of large establishments, employing a number of work-people, in the neighbourhood of Manchester; and, in every case, by the steady application of certain general principles, he succeeded in reforming the habits of those under his care, and who always, among their associates in similar employment, appeared conspicuous for their good conduct. With this previous success in remodeling English character, but ignorant of the local ideas, manners, and customs, of those now committed to his management, the stranger commenced his task.

At that time the lower classes in Scotland, like those of other countries, had strong prejudices against strangers having any authority over them, and particularly against the English, few of whom had then settled in Scotland, and not one in the neighbourhood of the scenes under description. It is also well known that even the Scotch peasantry and working classes possess the habit of making observations and reasoning thereon with great acuteness; and in the present case those employed naturally concluded that the new purchasers intended merely to make the utmost profit by the establishment, from the abuses of which many of themselves were then deriving support. The persons employed at these works were therefore strongly prejudiced against the new director of the establishment,—prejudiced, because he was a stranger, and from England,—because he succeeded Mr. Dale, under whose proprietorship they acted almost as they liked,—because his religious creed was not theirs,—and because they concluded that the works would be governed by new laws and regulations, calculated to squeeze, as they often termed it, the greatest sum of gain out of their labour.

In consequence, from the day he arrived amongst them every means which ingenuity could devise was set to work to counteract the plan which he attempted to introduce; and for two years it was a regular attack and defence of prejudices and mal-practices between the manager and the population of the place, without the former being able to make much progress, or to convince the latter of the sincerity of his good intentions for their welfare. He, however, did not lose his patience, his temper, or his confidence in the certain success of the principles on which he founded his conduct.

These principles ultimately prevailed: the population could not continue to resist a firm well-directed kindness, administering justice to all. They therefore slowly and cautiously began to give him some portion of their confidence; and as this increased, he was enabled more and more to develop his plans for their amelioration. It may with truth be said, that at this period they possessed almost all the vices and very few of the virtues of a social community. Theft and the receipt of stolen goods was their trade, idleness and drunkenness their habit, falsehood and deception their garb, dissensions, civil and religious, their daily practice; they united only in a zealous systematic opposition to their employers.

Here then was a fair field on which to try the efficacy in practice of principles supposed capable of altering any characters. The manager formed his plans accordingly. He spent some time in finding out the full extent of the evil against which he had to contend, and in tracing the true causes which had produced and were continuing those effects. He found that all was distrust, disorder, and disunion; and he wished to introduce confidence, regularity, and harmony. He therefore began to bring forward his various expedients to withdraw the unfavourable circumstances by which they had hitherto been surrounded, and to replace them by others calculated to produce a more happy result. He soon discovered that theft was extended through almost all the ramifications of the community, and the receipt of stolen goods through all the country around. To remedy this evil, not one legal punishment was inflicted, not one individual imprisoned, even for an hour; but checks and other regulations of prevention were introduced; a short plain explanation of the immediate benefits they would derive from a different conduct was inculcated by those instructed for the purpose, who had the best powers of reasoning among themselves. They were at the same time instructed how to direct their industry in legal and useful occupations, by which, without danger or disgrace, they could really earn more than they had previously obtained by dishonest practices. Thus the difficulty of committing the crime was increased, the detection afterwards rendered more easy, the habit of honest industry formed, and the pleasure of good conduct experienced.

Drunkenness was attacked in the same manner; it was discountenanced on every occasion by those who had charge of any department: its destructive and pernicious effects were frequently stated by his own more prudent comrades, at the proper moment when the individual was soberly suffering from the effects of his previous excess; pot and public houses were gradually removed from the immediate vicinity of their dwellings; the health and comfort of temperance were made familiar to them: by degrees drunkenness disappeared, and many who were habitual bacchanalians are now conspicuous for undeviating sobriety.

Falsehood and deception met with a similar fate: they were held in disgrace: their practical evils were shortly explained; and every countenance was given to truth and open conduct. The pleasure and substantial advantages derived from the latter soon overcame the impolicy, error, and consequent misery, which the former mode of acting had created.

Dissensions and quarrels were undermined by analogous expedients. When they could not be readily adjusted between the parties themselves, they were stated to the manager; and as in such cases both disputants were usually more or less in the wrong, that wrong was in as few words as possible explained, forgiveness and friendship recommended, and one simple and easily remembered precept inculcated, as the most valuable rule for their whole conduct, and the advantages of which they would experience every moment of their lives; viz:—"That in future they should endeavour to use the same active exertions to make each other happy and comfortable, as they had hitherto done to make each other miserable; and by carrying this short memorandum in their mind, and applying it on all occasions, they would soon render that place a paradise, which, from the most mistaken principle of action, they now made the abode of misery." The experiment was tried: the parties enjoyed the gratification of this new mode of conduct; references rapidly subsided; and now serious differences are scarcely known.

Considerable jealousies also existed on account of one religious sect possessing a decided preference over the others. This was corrected by discontinuing that preference, and by giving an uniform encouragement to those who conducted themselves well among all the various religious persuasions; by recommending the same consideration to be shown to the conscientious opinions of each sect, on the ground that all must believe the particular doctrines which they had been taught, and consequently that all were in that respect upon an equal footing, nor was it possible yet to say which was right or wrong. It was likewise inculcated that all should attend to the essence of religion, and not act as the world was now taught and trained to do; that is, to overlook the substance and essence of religion, and devote their talents, time, and money, to that which is far worse than its shadow, sectarianism; another term for something very injurious to society, and very absurd, which one or other well-meaning enthusiast has added to *true religion*, which, without these defects, would soon form those characters which every wise and good man is anxious to see.

Such statements and conduct arrested sectarian animosity and ignorant intolerance; each retains full liberty of conscience, and in consequence each partakes of the sincere friendship of many sects instead of one. They act with cordiality together in the same departments and pursuits, and associate as though the whole community were not of different sectarian persuasions; and not one evil ensues.

The same principles were applied to correct the irregular intercourse of the sexes:—such conduct was discountenanced and held in disgrace; fines were levied upon both parties for the use of the support fund of the community. (This fund arose from each individual contributing one-sixtieth part of their wages, which, under their management, was applied to support the sick, the injured by accident, and the aged.) But because they had once unfortunately offended against the established laws and customs of society, they were not forced to become vicious, abandoned, and miserable; the door was left open for them to return to the comforts of kind friends and respected acquaintances; and, beyond any previous expectation, the evil became greatly diminished.

The system of receiving apprentices from public charities was abolished; permanent settlers with large families were encouraged, and comfortable houses were built for their accommodation.

The practice of employing children in the mills, of six, seven, and eight years of age, was discontinued, and their parents advised to allow them to acquire health and education until they were ten years old. (It may be remarked, that even this age is too early to keep them at constant employment in manufactories, from six in the morning to seven in the evening. Far better would it be for the children, their parents, and for society, that the first should not commence employment until they attain the age of twelve, when their education might be finished, and their bodies would be more competent to undergo the fatigue and exertions required of them. When parents can be trained to afford this additional time to their children without inconvenience, they will, of course, adopt the practice now recommended.)

The children were taught reading, writing, and arithmetic, during five years, that is, from five to ten, in the village school, without expense to their parents. All the modern improvements in education have been adopted, or are in process of adoption. (To avoid the inconveniences which must ever arise from the introduction of a particular creed into a school, the children are taught to read in such books as inculcate those precepts of the Christian religion, which are common to all denominations.) They may therefore be taught and well-trained before they engage in any regular employment. Another important consideration is, that all their instruction is rendered a pleasure and delight to them; they are much more anxious for the hour of school-time to arrive than to end; they therefore make a rapid progress; and it may be safely asserted, that if they shall not be trained to

A New View of Society

form such characters as may be most desired, the fault will not proceed from the children; the cause will be in the want of a true knowledge of human nature in those who have the management of them and their parents.

During the period that these changes were going forward, attention was given to the domestic arrangements of the community.

Their houses were rendered more comfortable, their streets were improved, the best provisions were purchased, and sold to them at low rates, yet covering the original expense, and under such regulations as taught them how to proportion their expenditure to their income. Fuel and clothes were obtained for them in the same manner; and no advantage was attempted to be taken of them, or means used to deceive them.

In consequence, their animosity and opposition to the stranger subsided, their full confidence was obtained, and they became satisfied that no evil was intended them, they were convinced that a real desire existed to increase their happiness upon those grounds alone on which it could be permanently increased. All difficulties in the way of future improvement vanished. They were taught to be rational, and they acted rationally. Thus both parties experienced the incalculable advantages of the system which had been adopted. Those employed became industrious, temperate, healthy, faithful to their employers, and kind to each other; while the proprietors were deriving services from their attachment, almost without inspection, far beyond those which could be obtained by any other means than those of mutual confidence and kindness. Such was the effect of these principles on the adults; on those whose previous habits had been as ill-formed as habits could be: and certainly the application of the principles to practice was made under the most unfavourable circumstances. (It may be supposed that this community was separated from other society; but the supposition would be erroneous, for it had daily and hourly communication with a population exceeding its own number. The royal borough of Lanark is only one mile distant from the works; many individuals came daily from the former to be employed at the latter; and a general intercourse is constantly maintained between the old and new towns.)

I have thus given a detailed account of this experiment, although a partial application of the principles is of far less importance than a clear and accurate account of the principles themselves, in order that they may be so well understood as to be easily rendered applicable to practice in any community and under any circumstances. Without this, particular facts may indeed amuse or astonish, but they would not contain that substantial value which the principles will be found to possess. But if the relation of the narrative shall forward this object, the experiment cannot fail to prove the certain means of renovating the moral and religious principles of the world, by showing whence arise the various opinions, manners, vices, and virtues of mankind, and how the best or the worst of them may, with mathematical precision, be taught to the rising generation.

Let it not, therefore, be longer said that evil or injurious actions cannot be prevented, or that the most rational habits in the rising generation cannot be universally formed. In those characters which now exhibit crime, the fault is obviously not in the individual, but the defects proceed from the system in which the individual was trained. Withdraw those circumstances which tend to create crime in the human character, and crime will not be created. Replace them with such as

A New View of Society 71

are calculated to form habits of order, regularity, temperance, industry; and these qualities will be formed. Adopt measures of fair equity and justice, and you will readily acquire the full and complete confidence of the lower orders. Proceed systematically on principles of undeviating persevering kindness, yet retaining and using, with the least possible severity, the means of restraining crime from immediately injuring society; and by degrees even the crimes now existing in the adults will also gradually disappear: for the worst formed disposition, short of incurable insanity, will not long resist a firm, determined, well-directed, persevering kindness. Such a proceeding, whenever practised, will be found the most powerful and effective corrector of crime, and of all injurious and improper habits.

The experiment narrated shows that this is not hypothesis and theory. The principles may be with confidence stated to be universal, and applicable to all times, persons, and circumstances. And the most obvious application of them would be to adopt rational means to remove the temptation to commit crimes, and increase the difficulties of committing them; while, at the same time, a proper direction should be given to the active powers of the individual; and a due share provided of uninjurious amusements and recreation. Care must also be taken to remove the causes of jealousy, dissensions, and irritation; to introduce sentiments calculated to create union and confidence among all the members of the community; and the whole should be directed by a persevering kindness, sufficiently evident to prove that a sincere desire exists to increase, and not to diminish, happiness.

These principles, applied to the community at New Lanark, at first under many of the most discouraging circumstances, but persevered in for sixteen years, effected a complete change in the general character of the village, containing upwards of two thousand inhabitants, and into which, also, there was a constant influx of new comers. But as the promulgation of new miracles is not for present times, it is not pretended that under such circumstances one and all are become wise and good; or, that they are free from error. But it may be truly stated, that they now constitute a very improved society; that their worst habits are gone, and that their minor ones will soon disappear under a continuance of the application of the same principles; that during the period mentioned, scarcely a legal punishment has been inflicted, or an application been made for parish funds by any individual among them. Drunkenness is not seen in their streets; and the children are taught and trained in the institution for forming their character without any punishment. The community exhibits the general appearance of industry, temperance, comfort, health, and happiness. These are and ever will be the sure and certain effects of the adoption of the principles explained; and these principles, applied with judgment, will effectually reform the most vicious community existing, and train the younger part of it to any character which may be desired; and that, too, much more easily on an extended than on a limited scale. To apply these principles, however, successfully to practice, both a comprehensive and a minute view muct be taken of the existing state of the society on which they are intended to operate. The causes of the most prevalent evils must be accurately traced, and those means which appear the most easy and simple should be immediately applied to remove them.

In this progress the smallest alteration, adequate to produce any good effect, should be made at one time;

A New View of Society

indeed, if possible, the change should be so gradual as to be almost imperceptible, yet always making a permanent advance in the desired improvements. By this procedure the most rapid practical progress will be obtained, because the inclination to resistence will be removed, and time will be given for reason to weaken the force of long-established injurious prejudices. The removal of the first evil will prepare the way for the removal of the second; and this facility will increase, not in an arithmetical, but in a geometrical proportion; until the directors of the system will themselves be gratified beyond expression with the beneficial magnitude of their own proceedings.

Nor while these principles shall be acted upon can there be any retrogression in this good work; for the permanence of the amelioration will be equal to its extent.

What then remains to prevent such a system from being immediately adopted into national practice? Nothing, surely, but a general destitution of the knowledge of the practice. For with the certain means of preventing crimes, can it be supposed that British legislators, as soon as these means shall be made evident, will longer withhold them from their fellow-subjects? No: I am persuaded that neither prince, ministers, parliament, nor any party in church or state, will avow inclination to act on principles of such flagrant injustice. Have they not on many occasions evinced a sincere and ardent desire to ameliorate the conditions of the subjects of the empire, when practicable means of amelioration were explained to them, which could be adopted without risking the safety of the state?

For some time to come there can be but one practicable, and therefore one rational reform, which without danger can be attempted in these realms; a reform in which all men and all parties may join—that is, a reform in the training and in the management of the poor, the ignorant, the untaught and untrained, or ill-taught and ill-trained, among the whole mass of British population; and a plain, simple, practicable plan which would not contain the least danger to any individual, or to any part of society, may be devised for that purpose.

That plan is a national, well-digested, unexclusive system for the formation of character and general amelioration of the lower orders. On the experience of a life devoted to the subject, I hesitate not to say, that the members of any community may by degrees be trained to live *without idleness, without poverty, without crime, and without punishment;* for each of these is the effect of error in the various systems prevalent throughout the world. *They are all necessary consequences of ignorance.*

Train any population rationally, and they will be rational. Furnish honest and useful employments to those so trained, and such employments they will greatly prefer to dishonest or injurious occupations. It is beyond all calculation the interest of every government to provide that training and that employment; and to provide both is easily practicable.

The first, as before stated, is to be obtained by a national system for the formation of character; the second, by governments preparing a reserve of employment for the surplus working classes, when the general demand for labour throughout the country is not equal to the full occupation of the whole: that employment to be on useful national objects from which the public may derive advantage equal to the expense which those works may require.

The national plan for the formation of character

should *include* all the modern improvements of education, without regard to the system of any one individual; and should not *exclude* the child of any one subject in the empire. Anything short of this would be an act of intolerance and injustice to the excluded, and of injury to society, so glaring and manifest, that I shall be deceived in the character of my countrymen if any of those who have influence in church and state should now be found willing to attempt it. Is it not indeed strikingly evident even to common observers, that any further effort to enforce religious exclusion would involve the certain and speedy destruction of the present church establishment, and would even endanger our civil institutions?

It may be said, however, that ministers and parliament have many other important subjects under discussion. This is evidently true; but will they not have high national concerns always to engage their attention? And can any question be brought forward of deeper interest to the community than that which affects the formation of character and the well-being of every individual within the empire? A question, too, which, when understood, will be found to offer the means of amelioration to the revenues of these kingdoms, far beyond any practical plan now likely to be devised. Yet, important as are considerations of revenue, they must appear secondary when put in competition with the lives, liberty, and comfort of our fellow-subjects; which are now hourly sacrificed for want of an *effective legislative measure to prevent crime*. And is an act of such vital importance to the well-being of all to be longer delayed? *Shall yet another year pass in which crime shall be forced on the infant, who in ten, twenty, or thirty years hence shall suffer* DEATH *for being taught that crime?* Surely it is impossible. Should it be so delayed, *the individuals of the present parliament, the legislators of this day,* ought in strict and impartial justice to be amenable to the laws for not adopting the means in their power to prevent the crime; rather than the poor, untrained, and unprotected culprit, whose previous years, if he had language to describe them, would exhibit a life of unceasing wretchedness, arising *solely* from the errors of society.

Much might be added on these momentous subjects, even to make them evident to the capacities of children: but for obvious reasons the outlines are merely sketched; and it is hoped these outlines will be sufficient to induce the well-disposed of all parties cordially to unite in this vital measure for the preservation of every thing dear to society. . . .

Third Essay

. . . From the earliest ages it has been the practice of the world to act on the supposition that each individual man forms his own character, and that therefore he is accountable for all his sentiments and habits, and consequently merits reward for some and punishment for others. Every system which has been established among men has been founded on these erroneous principles. When, however, they shall be brought to the test of fair examination, they will be found not only unsupported, but in direct opposition to all experience, and to the evidence of our senses.

This is not a slight mistake, which involves only trivial consequences; it is a fundamental error of the highest possible magnitude; it enters into all our proceedings regarding man from his infancy; and it will be found to be the true and sole origin of evil. It generates and perpetuates ignorance, hatred, and revenge, where, without such error, only intelligence, confidence, and kindness, would exist. It has hitherto been the Evil Genius of the world. It severs man from man throughout the various regions of the earth; and makes enemies of those who, but for this gross error, would have enjoyed each other's kind offices and sincere friendship. It is, in short, an error which carries misery in all its consequences.

This error cannot much longer exist; for every day will make it more and more evident *that the character of man, is, without a single exception, always formed for him; that it may be, and is, chiefly, created by his predecessors; that they give him, or may give him, his ideas and habits, which are the powers that govern and direct his conduct. Man, therefore, never did, nor is it possible he ever can, form his own character.*

The knowledge of this important fact has not been derived from any of the wild and heated speculations of an ardent and ungoverned imagination; on the contrary, it proceeds from a long and patient study of the theory and practice of human nature, under many varied circumstances; it will be found to be a deduction drawn from such a multiplicity of facts, as to afford the most complete demonstration.

Had not mankind been mis-instructed from infancy on this subject, making it necessary that they should unlearn what they have been taught, the simple statement of this truth would render it instantly obvious to every rational mind. Men would know that their predecessors might have given them the habits of ferocious cannibalism, or of the highest known benevolence and intelligence; and by the acquirement of this knowledge they would soon learn that, as parents, preceptors, and legislators united, they possess the means of training the rising generations to either of those extremes; that they may with the greatest certainty make them the conscientious worshippers of Juggernaut, or of the most pure spirit, possessing the essence of every excellence which the human imagination can conceive; that they may train the young to become effeminate, deceitful, ignorantly selfish, intemperate, revengeful, murderous,—of course ignorant, irrational, and miserable; or to be manly, just, generous, temperate, active, kind, and benevolent,—that is intelligent, rational, and happy. The knowledge of these principles having been derived from facts which perpetually exist, they defy ingenuity itself to confute them; nay, the most severe scrutiny will make it evident that they are utterly unassailable.

Is it then wisdom to think and to act in opposition to the facts which hourly exhibit themselves around us, and in direct contradiction to the evidence of our senses? Inquire of the most learned and wise of the present day, ask them to speak with sincerity, and they will tell you that they have long known the principles on which society has been founded to be false. Hitherto, however, the tide of public opinion, in all countries, has been directed by a combination of prejudice, bigotry, and fanaticism, derived from the wildest imaginations of ignorance; and the most enlightened men have not dared to expose those errors which to them were offensive, prominent, and glaring.

Happily for man this reign of ignorance rapidly approaches to dissolution; its terrors are already on the wing, and soon they will be compelled to take their flight, never more to return. For now the knowledge of the existing errors is not only possessed by the learned and reflecting, but it is spreading far and wide throughout society; and ere long it will be fully comprehended even by the most ignorant.

Attempts may indeed be made by individuals, who through ignorance mistake their real interests, to retard the progress of this knowledge; but as it will prove itself to be in unison with the evidence of our senses, and therefore true beyond the possibility of disproof, it cannot be impeded, and in its course will overwhelm all opposition.

These principles, however, are not more true in theory than beneficial in practice, whenever they are properly applied. Why, then, should all their substantial advantages be longer withheld from the mass of mankind? Can it, by possibility, be a crime to pursue the only practical means which a rational being can adopt to diminish the misery of man, and increase his happiness?

These questions, of the deepest interest to society, are now brought to the fair test of public experiment. It remains to be proved, whether the character of man shall continue to be formed under the guidance of the most inconsistent notions, the errors of which for centuries past have been manifest to every reflecting rational mind; or whether it shall be moulded under the direction of uniformly consistent principles, derived from the unvarying facts of the creation; principles, the truth of which no sane man will now attempt to deny.

It is then by the full and complete disclosure of these principles, that the destruction of ignorance and misery is to be effected, and the reign of reason, intelligence, and happiness, is to be firmly established....

2. Robert Owen: The Institution for the Formation of Character

Opposition from his partners for some years prevented Owen from extending and remodeling the schools at New Lanark as he wished. But after a reorganization of the partnership he was able to go ahead with his ambitious Institution for the Formation of Character. The following Address . . . to the Inhabitants of New Lanark *(London, 1816) was delivered at the opening of the Institution in January 1816.*

We have met to-day for the purpose of opening this Institution; and it is my intention to explain to you the objects for which it has been founded.

These objects are most important.

The first relates to the immediate comfort and benefit of all the inhabitants of this village.

The second, to the welfare and advantage of the neighbourhood.

The third, to extensive ameliorations throughout the British dominions.

The last, to the gradual improvement of every nation in the world.

I will briefly explain how this Institution is to contribute towards producing these effects.

Long before I came to reside among you, it had been my chief study to discover the extent, causes, and rem-

The Institution for the Formation of Character

edy of the inconveniences and miseries which were perpetually recurring to every class in society.

The history of man informed me that innumerable attempts had been made, through every age, to lessen these evils; and experience convinced me that the present generation, stimulated by an accession of knowledge derived from past times, was eagerly engaged in the same pursuit. My mind at a very early period took a similar direction; and I became ardently desirous of investigating to its source a subject which involved the happiness of every human being.

It soon appeared to me, that the only path to knowledge on this subject had been neglected; that one leading in an opposite direction had alone been followed; that while causes existed to compel mankind to pursue such direction, it was idle to expect any successful result: and experience proves how vain their pursuit has been.

In this inquiry, men have hitherto been directed by their inventive faculties, and have almost entirely disregarded the only guide that can lead to true knowledge on any subject—experience. They have been governed, in the most important concerns of life, by mere illusions of the imagination, in direct opposition to existing facts.

Having satisfied myself beyond doubt with regard to this fundamental error; having traced the ignorance and misery which it has inflicted on man, by a calm and patient investigation of the causes which have continued this evil, without any intermission from one generation to another; and having also maturely reflected on the obstacles to be overcome, before a new direction can be given to the human mind; I was induced to form the resolution of devoting my life to relieve mankind from this mental disease and all its miseries.

It was evident to me that the evil was universal; that,

in practice, none was in the right path—no, not one; and that, in order to remedy the evil, a different one must be pursued. That the whole man must be re-formed on fundamental principles the very reverse of those in which he had been trained; in short, that the minds of all men must be born again, and their knowledge and practice commence on a new foundation.

Satisfied of the futility of the existing modes of instruction, and of the errors of the existing modes of government, I was well convinced that none of them could ever effect the ends intended; but that, on the contrary, they were only calculated to defeat all the objects which human instructors and governors had proposed to attain.

I found, on such a patient consideration of the subject as its importance demanded, that to reiterate precept upon precept, however excellent in theory, while no decisive measures were adopted to place mankind under circumstances in which it might be possible to put those precepts in practice, was but a waste of time. I therefore determined to form arrangements preparatory to the introduction of truths, the knowledge of which should dissipate the errors and evils of all the existing political and religious systems.

Be not alarmed at the magnitude of the attempt which this declaration opens to your view. Each change, as it occurs, will establish a substantial and permanent good, unattended by any counteracting evil; nor can the mind of man, formed on the old system, longer interpose obstacles capable of retarding the progress of those truths which I am now about to unfold to you. The futile attempts which ignorance may for a short time oppose to them, will be found to accelerate their introduction. As soon as they shall be comprehended in all their bearings, every one will be compelled to acknowledge them, to see their benefits in practice to himself and to each of his fellow-creatures; for, by this system, none, no not one, will be injured. It is a delightful thought, an animating reflection, a stimulus to the steady prosecution of my purpose, beyond—nay, far beyond—all that riches, and honour, and praise can bestow, to be conscious of the possibility of being instrumental in introducing a practical system into society, the complete establishment of which *shall give happiness to every human being through all succeeding generations.* And such I declare was the sole motive that gave rise to this Institution, and to all my proceedings.

To effect any permanently beneficial change in society, I found it was far more necessary to *act* than to *speak.* I tried the effect of the new principles on a limited scale in the southern part of the Island. The result exceeded my most sanguine anticipations; and I became anxious for a more enlarged field of action. I saw New Lanark: it possessed many of the local circumstances proper for my purpose; and this establishment became at my disposal. This event, as many of you may recollect, occurred upwards of sixteen years ago. Sixteen years of action is not a short period: extensive changes are the result. You have been witnesses of my proceedings here, from the time I undertook the direction of the establishment to the present hour. I now ask, and I will thank you to make either a public or a private reply,—have any of you discovered even *one* of my measures that was not clearly and decisively intended to benefit the whole population? But I am satisfied that you are now convinced of this truth. You also know some of the obstacles which were opposed to my progress; but you know not a tithe of them. Yet, after all, these obstacles have been few, compared with those which I expected and was prepared to meet; and which I trust I should have overcome.

When I examined the circumstances under which I found you, they appeared to me to be very similar to those of other manufacturing districts; except with regard to the boarding-house, which contained the young children who were procured from the public charities of the country. That part of the establishment was under an admirable arrangement, and was a strong indication of the genuine and extensive benevolence of the revered and truly good man, (the late David Dale of Glasgow,) who founded these works and this village. His wishes and intentions towards you all were those of a father towards his children. You knew him and his worth; and his memory must be deeply engraven upon your hearts. Little indeed could he be conscious when he laid the first stone of this establishment, that he was commencing a work, from whence not only the amelioration of his suffering countrymen should proceed, but the means of happiness be developed to every nation in the world.

I have stated that I found the population of this place similar to that of other manufacturing districts. It was, with some exceptions, existing in poverty, crime, and misery; and strongly prejudiced, as most people are at first, against any change that might be proposed. The usual mode of proceeding on the principles which have hitherto governed the conduct of men, would have been to punish those who committed the crimes, and to be highly displeased with every one who opposed the alterations that were intended for his benefit. The principles, however, upon which the new system is founded, lead to a very different conduct. They make it evident, that when men are in poverty,—when they commit crimes or actions injurious to themselves and others,—and

The Institution for the Formation of Character

when they are in a state of wretchedness,—there must be substantial causes for these lamentable effects; and that, instead of punishing or being angry with our fellow-men because they have been subjected to such a miserable existence, we ought to pity and commiserate them, and patiently to trace the causes whence the evils proceed, and endeavour to discover whether they may not be removed.

This was the course which I adopted. I sought not the punishment of any delinquent, nor felt anger at your conduct in opposition to your own good; and when apparently stern and decisive, I was not actuated by a single feeling of irritation against any individual. I dispassionately investigated the source of the evils with which I saw you afflicted. The immediate causes of them were soon obvious; nor were the remote ones, or the causes of those causes, long hid from me.

I found that those which principally produced your misery, were practices you had been permitted to acquire —of falsehood, of theft, of drunkenness, of injustice in your transactions, want of charity for the opinions of others, and mistaken notions, in which you had been instructed, as to the superiority of your religious opinions, and that these were calculated to produce more happiness than any of the opinions impressed on the minds of an infinitely more numerous part of mankind. I found, also, that these causes were but the effects of others; and that those others might all be traced to the ignorance in which our forefathers existed, and in which we ourselves have continued to this day.

But from this day a change must take place; a new era must commence; the human intellect, through the whole extent of the earth, hitherto enveloped by the grossest ignorance and superstition, must begin to be released from its state of darkness; nor shall nourishment henceforth be given to the seeds of disunion and division among men. For the time is come, when the means may be prepared to train all the nations of the world—men of every colour and climate, of the most diversified habits—in that knowledge which shall impel them not only to love but to be actively kind to each other in the whole of their conduct, without a single exception. I speak not an unmeaning jargon of words, but that which I know—that which has been derived from a cool and dispassionate examination and comparison, during a quarter of a century, of the facts which exist around us. And, however averse men may be to resign their early-taught prejudices, I pledge myself to prove, to the entire satisfaction of the world, the truth of all that I have stated and all that I mean to state. Nay, such is my confidence in the truth of the principles on which the system I am about to introduce is founded, that I hesitate not to assert their power heartily to incline all men to say, "This system is assuredly true, and therefore eminently calculated to realise those invaluable precepts of the Gospel—universal charity, good will, and peace among men. Hitherto we must have been trained in error; and we hail it as the harbinger of that period when our swords shall be turned into plough-shares, and our spears into pruning-hooks; when universal love and benevolence shall prevail; when there shall be but one language and one nation; and when fear of want or of any evil among men shall be known no more."

Acting, although unknown to you, uniformly and steadily upon this system, my attention was ever directed to remove, as I could prepare means for their removal, such of the immediate causes as were perpetually creating misery amongst you, and which, if permitted to re-

The Institution for the Formation of Character 87

main, would to this day have continued to create misery. I therefore withdrew the most prominent incitements to falsehood, theft, drunkenness, and other pernicious habits, with which many of you were then familiar: and in their stead I introduced other causes, which were intended to produce better external habits; and better external habits have been introduced. I say better *external* habits; for to these alone have my proceedings hitherto been intended to apply. What has yet been done I consider as merely preparatory.

This Institution, when all its parts shall be completed, is intended to produce permanently beneficial effects; and, instead of longer applying temporary expedients for correcting some of your most prominent external habits, to effect a complete and thorough improvement in the *internal* as well as *external* character of the whole village. For this purpose the Institution has been devised to afford the means of receiving your children at an early age, as soon almost as they can walk. By this means many of you, mothers of families, will be enabled to earn a better maintenance or support for your children; you will have less care and anxiety about them; while the children will be prevented from acquiring any bad habits, and gradually prepared to learn the best.

The middle room of the story below will be appropriated to their accommodation; and in this their chief occupation will be to play and amuse themselves in severe weather: at other times they will be permitted to occupy the enclosed area before the building; for, to give children a vigorous constitution, they ought to be kept as much as possible in the open air. As they advance in years, they will be taken into the rooms on the right and left, where they will be regularly instructed in the rudiments of common learning; which, before they shall be six years old, they may be taught in a superior manner.

These stages may be called the first and second preparatory schools: and when your children shall have passed through them, they will be admitted into this place, (intended also to be used as a chapel,) which, with the adjoining apartment, is to be the general school-room for reading, writing, arithmetic, sewing, and knitting; all which, on the plan to be pursued, will be accomplished to a considerable extent by the time the children are ten years old; before which age, none of them will be permitted to enter the works.

For the benefit of the health and spirits of the children both boys and girls will be taught to dance, and the boys will be instructed in military exercises; those of each sex who may have good voices will be taught to sing, and those among the boys who have a taste for music will be taught to play upon some instrument; for it is intended to give them as much diversified innocent amusement as the local circumstances of the establishment will admit.

The rooms to the east and west on the story below, will also be appropriated in bad weather for relaxation and exercise during some part of the day, to the children who, in the regular hours of teaching, are to be instructed in these apartments.

In this manner is the Institution to be occupied during the day in winter. In summer, it is intended that they shall derive knowledge from a personal examination of the works of nature and of art, by going out frequently with some of their masters into the neighbourhood and country around.

After the instruction of the children who are too young to attend the works shall have been finished for the day, the apartments shall be cleaned, ventilated,

The Institution for the Formation of Character

and in winter lighted and heated, and in all respects made comfortable, for the reception of other classes of the population. The apartments on this floor are then to be appropriated for the use of the children and youth of both sexes who have been employed at work during the day, and who may wish still further to improve themselves in reading, writing, arithmetic, sewing, or knitting; or to learn any of the useful arts: to instruct them in which, proper masters and mistresses, who are appointed, will attend for two hours every evening.

The three lower rooms, which in winter will also be well lighted and properly heated, will be thrown open for the use of the adult part of the population, who are to be provided with every accommodation requisite to enable them to read, write, account, sew, or play, converse, or walk about. But strict order and attention to the happiness of every one of the party will be enforced, until such habits shall be acquired as will render any formal restriction unnecessary; and the measures thus adopted will soon remove such necessity.

Two evenings in the week will be appropriated to dancing and music: but on these occasions every accommodation will be prepared for those who prefer to study or to follow any of the occupations pursued on the other evenings.

One of the apartments will also be occasionally appropriated for the purpose of giving useful instruction to the older classes of the inhabitants. For, believe me, my friends, you are yet very deficient with regard to the best modes of training your children, or of arranging your domestic concerns; as well as in that wisdom which is requisite to direct your conduct towards each other, so as to enable you to become greatly more happy than you have ever yet been. There will be no difficulty in teaching you what is right and proper; your own interests will afford ample stimulus for that purpose; but the real and only difficulty will be to unlearn those pernicious habits and sentiments which an infinite variety of causes, existing through all past ages, have combined to impress upon your minds and bodies, so as to make you imagine that they are inseparable from your nature. It shall, however, ere long be proved to you, that in this respect, as well as in many others, you and all mankind are mistaken. Yet think not, from what I have said, that I mean to infringe, even in the most slight degree, on the liberty of private judgment or religious opinions. No! they have hitherto been unrestrained; and the most effectual measures have been adopted by all the parties interested in the concern, to secure to you these most invaluable privileges. And here I now publicly declare, (and while I make the declaration I wish my voice could extend to the ear, and make its due impression on the mind, of every one of our fellow-creatures,) "that the individual who first placed restraint on private judgment and religious opinions, was the author of hypocrisy, and the origin of innumerable evils which mankind through every past age have experienced." The right, however, of private judgment, and of real religious liberty, is nowhere yet enjoyed. It is not possessed by any nation in the world; and thence the unnecessary ignorance, as well as endless misery, of all. Nor can this right be enjoyed until the principle whence opinions originate shall be universally known and acknowledged.

The chief object of my existence will be to make this knowledge universal, and thence to bring the right of private judgment into general practice; to show the infinitely beneficial consequences that will result to mankind from its adoption. To effect this important purpose is a part, and an essential part, of that system which is about to be introduced.

I proceed to show how the Institution is to contribute to the welfare and advantage of this neighbourhood.

It will be readily admitted, that a population trained in regular habits of temperance, industry, and sobriety; of genuine charity for the opinions of all mankind, founded on the only knowledge that can implant true charity in the breast of any human being; trained also in a sincere desire to do good to the utmost of their power, and without any exception, to every one of their fellow-creatures, cannot, even by their example alone, do otherwise than materially increase the welfare and advantages of the neighbourhood in which such a population may be situated. To feel the due weight of this consideration, only imagine to yourselves 2,000 or 3,000 human beings trained in habits of licentiousness, and allowed to remain in gross ignorance. How much, in such a case, would not the peace, quiet, comfort, and happiness of the neighbourhood be destroyed! But there is not anything I have done, or purpose to do, which is not intended to benefit my fellow-creatures to the greatest extent that my operations can embrace. I wish to benefit all equally; but circumstances limit my present measures for the public good within a narrow circle. I must begin to act at some point; and a combination of singular events has fixed that point at this establishment. The first and greatest advantages will therefore centre here. But, in unison with the principle thus stated, it has ever been my intention that as this institution, when completed, will accommodate more than the children of parents resident at the village, any persons living at Lanark, or in the neighbourhood anywhere around, who cannot well afford to educate their children, shall be at liberty, on mentioning their wishes, to send them to this place, where they will experience the same care and attention as those who belong to the establishment. Nor will there be any distinction made between the children of those parents who are deemed the worst, and of those who may be esteemed the best, members of society: rather, indeed, would I prefer to receive the offspring of the worst, if they shall be sent at an early age; because they really require more of our care and pity; and by well-training these, society will be more essentially benefited, than if the like attention were paid to those whose parents are educating them in comparatively good habits. The system now preparing, and which will ultimately be brought into full practice, is to effect a complete change in all our sentiments and conduct towards those poor miserable creatures whom the errors of past times have denominated the bad, the worthless, and the wicked. A more enlarged and better knowledge of human nature will make it evident that, in strict justice, those who apply these terms to their fellow men are not only the most ignorant, but are themselves the immediate causes of more misery in the world than those whom they call the outcasts of society. *They* are, therefore, correctly speaking, the most wicked and worthless; and were they not grossly deceived, and rendered blind from infancy, they would become conscious of the lamentably extensive evils, which, by their well-intended but most mistaken conduct, they have, during so long a period, inflicted on their fellow men. But the veil of darkness must be removed from their eyes; their erroneous proceedings must be made so palpable that they shall thenceforth reject them with horror. Yes! they will reject with horror even those notions which hitherto they have from infancy been taught to value beyond price.

The Institution for the Formation of Character

To that which follows I wish to direct the attention of all your faculties. I am about to declare to you the cause and the cure of that which is called wickedness in your fellow men. As we proceed, instead of your feelings being roused to hate and to pursue them to punishment, you will be compelled to pity them; to commiserate their condition; nay, to love them, and to be convinced that to this day they have been treated unkindly, unjustly, and with the greatest cruelty. It is indeed high time, my friends, that our conduct—that the conduct of all mankind, in this respect, should be the very reverse of what it has been; and of this truth, new as it may and must appear to many of you, you shall, as I proceed, be satisfied to the most complete conviction.

That, then, which has been hitherto called wickedness in our fellow men, has proceeded from one of two distinct causes, or from some combination of those causes. They are what is termed bad or wicked,—

1st,—Because they are born with faculties and propensities which render them more liable, under the circumstances, than other men, to commit such actions as are usually denominated wicked. Or

2nd,—Because they have been placed, by birth or by other events, in particular countries; have been influenced from infancy by parents, playmates, and others; and have been surrounded by those circumstances which gradually and necessarily trained them in the habits and sentiments called wicked. Or

3rd,—They have become wicked in consequence of some particular combination of these causes.

Let us now examine them separately, and endeavour to discover whether any, and which of them, have originated with the individuals; and, of course, for which of them they ought to be treated by their fellow men in the manner those denominated wicked have to this day been treated.

You have not, I trust, been rendered so completely insane, by the ignorance of our forefathers, as to imagine that the poor helpless infant, devoid of understanding, made itself, or any of its bodily or mental faculties or qualities: but, whatever you may have been taught, it is a fact, that every infant has received all its faculties and qualities, bodily and mental, from a power and cause, over which the infant had not the shadow of control.

Shall it, then, be unkindly treated? And, when it shall be grown up, shall it be punished with loss of liberty or life, because a power over which it had no control whatever, formed it in the womb with faculties and qualities different from those of its fellows?—Has the infant any means of deciding who, or of what description, shall be its parents, its playmates, or those from whom it shall derive its habits and its sentiments?—Has it the power to determine for itself whether it shall first see light within the circle of Christendom; or whether it shall be so placed as inevitably to become a disciple of Moses, of Confucius, of Mahomed; a worshipper of the great idol Juggernaut, or a savage and a cannibal?

If then, my friends, not even one of these great leading and overwhelming circumstances can be, in the smallest degree, under the control of the infant, is there a being in existence, possessing any claim even to the smallest degree of rationality, who will maintain that any individual, formed and placed under such circumstances, ought to be punished, or in any respect unkindly treated? When men shall be in some degree relieved from the mental malady with which they have been so long afflicted, and sound judgment shall take the place of wild and senseless imagination, then the united voice of mankind shall say, "No!" And they will be astonished that a contrary supposition should ever have prevailed.

If it should be asked,—Whence, then, have wickedness and misery proceeded? I reply, *Solely from the ignorance of our forefathers!* It is this ignorance, my friends, that has been, and continues to be, the only cause of all the miseries which men have experienced. This is the evil spirit which has had dominion over the world,— which has sown the seeds of hatred and disunion among all nations,—which has grossly deceived mankind, by introducing notions the most absurd and unaccountable respecting faith and belief; notions by which it has effectually placed a seal on all the rational faculties of man,—by which numberless evil passions are engendered,—by which all men, in the most senseless manner, are not only made enemies to each other, but enemies to their own happiness! While this ignorance of our forefathers continues to abuse the world, under any name whatever, it is neither more nor less than a species of madness—rank insanity—to imagine that we can ever become in practice good, wise, or happy.

Were it not, indeed, for the positive evils which proceed from these senseless notions, they are too absurd to admit of a serious refutation; nor would any refutation be necessary, if they did not from infancy destroy the reasoning faculties of men, whether Pagans, Jews, Christians, or Mahomedans; and render them utterly incompetent to draw a just conclusion from the numberless facts which perpetually present themselves to notice. Do we not learn from history, that infants through all past ages have been taught the language, habits, and sentiments of those by whom they have been surrounded? That they had no means whatever of giving to themselves the power to acquire any others? That every generation has thought and acted like preceding generations, *with such changes only as the events around it, from which experience is derived, may have forced upon it?* And, above all, are we not conscious that the experience of every individual now existing is abundantly sufficient, on reflection, to prove to himself that he has no more power or command over his faith and belief than he possesses over the winds of heaven? nay, that his constitution is so formed, that in every instance whatsoever, the faith or belief which he possesses has been given to him by causes over which he had no control?

Experience, my friends, now makes these conclusions clear as the sun at noon-day. Why, then, shall we not instantly act upon them? Having discovered our error, why shall we longer afflict our fellow men with the evils which these wild notions have generated? Have they ever been productive of one benefit to mankind? Have they not produced, through all past ages—are they not at this moment engendering, every conceivable evil to which man, in every nation of the world, is subjected? Yes; these alone prevent the introduction of charity and universal good-will among men. These alone prevent men from discovering the true and only road which can lead to happiness. Once overcome these obstacles, and the apple of discord will be withdrawn from among us; the whole human race may then, with the greatest ease, be trained in one mind; all their efforts may then be trained to act for the good of the whole. In short, when these great errors shall be removed, all our evil passions will disappear; no ground of anger or displeasure from one human being towards another will remain; the period of the supposed Millennium will commence, and universal love prevail.

Will it not, then, tend to the welfare and advantage of

The Institution for the Formation of Character 97

this neighbourhood, to introduce into it such a practical system as shall gradually withdraw the causes of anger, hatred, discord, and every evil passion, and substitute true and genuine principles of universal charity and of never-varying kindness, of love without dissimulation, and of an ever-active desire to benefit to the full extent of our faculties all our fellow-creatures, whatever may be their sentiments and their habits,—wholly regardless whether they be Pagans, Jews, Christians, or Mahomedans? For anything short of this can proceed only from the evil spirit of ignorance, which is truly the roaring lion going about seeking whom he may devour.

We now come to the third division of the subject, which was to show that one of the objects of this Institution was to effect extensive ameliorations throughout the British dominions. This will be accomplished in two ways:—

1st,—By showing to the master manufacturers an example in practice, on a scale sufficiently extensive, of the mode by which the characters and situation of the working manufacturers whom they employ may be very materially improved, not only without injury to the masters, but so as to create to them also great and substantial advantages.

2nd,—By inducing, through this example, the British legislature to enact such laws as will secure similar benefits to every part of our population.

The extent of the benefits which may be produced by proper legislative measures, few are yet prepared to form any adequate idea of. By legislative measures I do not mean any party proceeding whatever. Those to which I allude are,—laws to diminish and ultimately prevent the most prominent evils to which the working classes are now subjected,—laws to prevent a large part of our fellow-subjects, under the manufacturing system, from being oppressed by a much smaller part,—to prevent more than one-half of our population from being trained in gross ignorance, and their valuable labour from being most injuriously directed,—laws to prevent the same valuable part of our population from being perpetually surrounded by temptations, which they have not been trained to resist, and which compel them to commit actions most hurtful to themselves and to society. The principles on which these measures are to be founded being once fairly and honestly understood, they will be easy of adoption; and the benefits to be derived from them in practice to every member of the community, will exceed any calculation that can be made by those not well versed in political economy.

These are some of the ameliorations which I trust this Institution will be the means of obtaining for our suffering fellow-subjects.

But, my friends, if what has been done, what is doing, and what has yet to be done here, should procure the benefits which I have imperfectly enumerated, to this village, to our neighbourhood, and to our country, only, I should be greatly disappointed; for I feel an ardent desire to benefit all my fellow men equally. I know not any distinction whatever. Political or religious parties or sects are everywhere the fruitful sources of disunion and irritation. My aim is therefore to withdraw the germ of all party from society. As little do I admit of the divisions and distinctions created by any imaginary lines which separate nation from nation. Will any being, entitled to the epithet intelligent, say that a mountain, a river, an ocean, or any shade of colour, or difference of climate, habits, and sentiments, affords a reason sufficient to satisfy the inquiries of even a well-trained child, why

The Institution for the Formation of Character

one portion of mankind should be taught to despise, hate, and destroy another? Are these absurd effects of the grossest ignorance never to be brought to a termination? Are we still to preserve and encourage the continuance of those errors which must inevitably make man an enemy to man? Are these the measures calculated to bring about that promised period when the lion shall lie down with the lamb, and when uninterrupted peace shall universally prevail?—peace, founded on a sincere good-will, instilled from infancy into the very constitution of every man, which is the only basis on which universal happiness can ever be established? I look, however, with the utmost confidence to the arrival of such a period; and, if proper measures shall be adopted, its date is not far distant.

What ideas individuals may attach to the term Millennium, I know not; but I know that society may be formed so as to exist without crime, without poverty, with health greatly improved, with little, if any, misery, and with intelligence and happiness increased a hundredfold; and no obstacle whatsoever intervenes at this moment, except ignorance, to prevent such a state of society from becoming universal.

I am aware, to the fullest extent, what various impressions these declarations will make on the different religious, political, learned, commercial, and other circles which compose the population of our empire. I know the particular shade of prejudice through which they will be presented to the minds of each of these. And to none will they appear through a denser medium than to the learned, who have been taught to suppose that the book of knowledge has been exclusively opened to them; while, in fact, they have only wasted their strength in wandering through endless mazes of error. They are totally ignorant of human nature. They are full of theories, and have not the most distant conception of what may or may not be accomplished in practice. It is true their minds have been well stored with language, which they can readily use to puzzle and confound the unlettered and inexperienced. But to those who have had an opportunity of examining the utmost extent of their acquirements, and of observing how far they have been taught, and where their knowledge terminates, the deception vanishes, and the fallacy of the foundation upon which the superstructure of all their acquirements has been raised, at once becomes most obvious. In short, with a few exceptions, their profound investigations have been about words only. For, as the principle which they have been taught, and on which all their subsequent instruction proceeds, is erroneous, so it becomes impossible that they can arrive at just conclusions. The learned have ever looked for the cause of human sentiments and actions in the individual through whom those sentiments and actions become visible,—and hitherto the learned have governed the opinions of the world. The individual has been praised, blamed, or punished, according to the whims and fancies of this class of men, and, in consequence, the earth has been full charged with their ever-varying absurdities, and with the miseries which these absurdities hourly create. Had it not been a law of our nature, that any impression, however ridiculous and absurd, and however contrary to fact, may be given in infancy, so as to be tenaciously retained through life, men could not have passed through the previous ages of the world without discovering the gross errors in which they had been trained. They could not have persevered in making each other miserable, and filling the world with horrors of every description. No!

The Institution for the Formation of Character

they would long since have discovered the natural, easy, and simple means of giving happiness to themselves and to every human being. But that law of nature which renders it difficult to eradicate our early instruction, although it will ultimately prove highly beneficial to the human race, serves now but to give permanence to error, and to blind our judgments. For the present situation of all the inhabitants of the earth may be compared to that of one whose eyes have been closely bandaged from infancy; who has afterwards been taught to imagine that he clearly sees the form or colour of every object around him; and who has been continually flattered with this notion, so as to compel his implicit belief in the supposition, and render him impenetrable to every attempt that could be made to undeceive him. If such be the present situation of man, how shall the illusion under which he exists be withdrawn from his mind? To beings thus circumstanced, what powers of persuasion can be applied, to make them comprehend their misfortune, and manifest to them the extent of the darkness in which they exist? In what language and in what manner shall the attempt be made? Will not every such attempt irritate and increase the malady, until means shall be devised to unloose the bandage, and thus effectually remove the cause of this mental blindness? Your minds have been so completely enveloped by this dense covering, which has intercepted the approach of every ray of light, that were an angel from heaven to descend and declare your state, you would not, because so circumstanced you could not, believe him.

Causes, over which I could have no control, removed in my early days the bandage which covered my mental sight. If I have been enabled to discover this blindness with which my fellow men are afflicted, to trace their wanderings from the path which they were most anxious to find, and at the same time to perceive that relief could not be administered to them by any premature disclosure of their unhappy state, it is not from any merit of mine; nor can I claim any personal consideration whatever for having been myself relieved from this unhappy situation. But, beholding such truly pitiable objects around me, and witnessing the misery which they hourly experienced from falling into the dangers and evils by which, in these paths, they were on every side surrounded,— could I remain an idle spectator? Could I tranquilly see my fellow men walking like idiots in every imaginable direction, except that alone in which the happiness they were in search of could be found?

No! The causes which fashioned me in the womb,— the circumstances by which I was surrounded from my birth, and over which I had no influence whatever, formed me with far other faculties, habits, and sentiments. These gave me a mind that could not rest satisfied without trying every possible expedient to relieve my fellow men from their wretched situation, and formed it of such a texture that obstacles of the most formidable nature served but to increase my ardour, and to fix within me a settled determination, either to overcome them, or to die in the attempt.

But the attempt has been made. In my progress the most multiplied difficulties, which to me at a distance seemed almost appalling, and which to others seemed absolutely insurmountable, have on their nearer approach diminished, until, at length, I have lived to see them disappear, like the fleeting clouds of morning, which prove but the harbingers of an animating and cheering day.

Hitherto I have not been disappointed in any of the

The Institution for the Formation of Character

expectations which I had formed. The events which have yet occurred far exceed my most sanguine anticipations, and my future course now appears evident and straightforward. It is no longer necessary that I should silently and alone exert myself for your benefit and the happiness of mankind. The period is arrived when I may call numbers to my aid, and the call will not be in vain. I well knew the danger which would arise from a premature and abrupt attempt to tear off the many-folded bandages of ignorance, which kept society in darkness. I have therefore been many years engaged, in a manner imperceptible to the public, in gently and gradually removing one fold after another of these fatal bands, from the mental eyes of those who have the chief influence in society. The principles on which the practical system I contemplate is to be founded, are now familiar to some of the leading men of all sects and parties in this country, and to many of the governing powers in Europe and America. They have been submitted to the examination of the most celebrated universities in Europe. They have been subjected to the minute scrutiny of the most learned and acute minds formed on the old system, and I am fully satisfied of their inability to disprove them. These principles I will shortly state.

Every society which exists at present, as well as every society which history records, has been formed and governed on a belief in the following notions, assumed as *first principles:*—

1st.—That it is in the power of every individual to form his own character.

Hence the various systems called by the name of religion, codes of law, and punishments. Hence also the angry passions entertained by individuals and nations towards each other.

2nd.—That the affections are at the command of the individual.

Hence insincerity and degradation of character. Hence the miseries of domestic life, and more than one-half of all the crimes of mankind.

3rd.—That it is necessary that a large portion of mankind should exist in ignorance and poverty, in order to secure to the remaining part such a degree of happiness as they now enjoy.

Hence a system of counteraction in the pursuits of men, a general opposition among individuals to the interests of each other, and the necessary effects of such a system,—ignorance, poverty, and vice.

Facts prove, however,

1st.—That character is universally formed *for,* and not *by*, the individual.

2nd.—That *any* habits and sentiments may be given to mankind.

3rd.—That the affections are *not* under the control of the individual.

4th.—That every individual may be trained to produce far more than he can consume, while there is a sufficiency of soil left for him to cultivate.

5th.—That nature has provided means by which populations may be at all times maintained in the proper state to give the greatest happiness to every individual, without one check of vice or misery.

6th.—That any community may be arranged, on a due combination of the foregoing principles, in such a manner, as not only to withdraw vice, poverty, and, in a great degree, misery, from the world, but also to place *every* individual under circumstances in which he shall enjoy more permanent happiness than can be given to *any* individual under the principles which have hitherto regulated society.

The Institution for the Formation of Character

7th.—That all the assumed fundamental principles on which society has hitherto been founded are erroneous, and may be demonstrated to be contrary to fact. And

8th.—That the change which would follow the abandonment of those erroneous maxims which bring misery into the world, and the adoption of principles of truth, unfolding a system which shall remove and for ever exclude that misery, may be effected without the slightest injury to any human being.

Here is the ground-work,—these are the data, on which society shall ere long be re-arranged; and for this simple reason, that it will be rendered evident that it will be for the immediate and future interest of every one to lend his most active assistance gradually to reform society on this basis. I say *gradually*, for in that word the most important considerations are involved. Any sudden and coercive attempt which may be made to remove even misery from men, will prove injurious rather than beneficial. Their minds must be gradually prepared by an essential alteration of the circumstances which surround them, for any great and important change and amelioration in their condition. They must be first convinced of their blindness: this cannot be effected, even among the least unreasonable, or those termed the best part of mankind, in their present state, without creating some degree of irritation. This irritation, must then be tranquilised before another step ought to be attempted; and a general conviction must be established of the truth of the principles on which the projected change is to be founded. Their introduction into practice will then become easy,—difficulties will vanish as we approach them,—and, afterwards, the desire to see the whole system carried immediately into effect will exceed the means of putting it into execution.

The principles on which this practical system is

founded are not new; separately, or partially united, they have been often recommended by the sages of antiquity, and by modern writers. But it is not known to me that they have ever been thus combined. Yet it can be demonstrated that it is only by their being *all brought into practice together,* that they are to be rendered beneficial to mankind; and sure I am that this is the earliest period in the history of man when they could be successfully introduced into practice.

I do not intend to hide from you that the change will be great. "Old things shall pass away, and all shall become new."

But this change will bear no resemblance to any of the revolutions which have hitherto occurred. These have been alone calculated to generate and call forth all the evil passions of hatred and revenge: but that system which is now contemplated will effectually eradicate every feeling of irritation and ill-will which exists among mankind. The whole proceedings of those who govern and instruct the world will be reversed. Instead of spending ages in telling mankind what they ought to think and how they ought to act, the instructors and governors of the world will acquire a knowledge that will enable them, in one generation, to apply the means which shall cheerfully induce each of those whom they control and influence, not only to think, but to act in such a manner as shall be best for himself and best for every human being. And yet this extraordinary result will take place without punishment or apparent force.

Under this system, before commands are issued it shall be known whether they can or cannot be obeyed. Men shall not be called upon to assent to doctrines and to dogmas which do not carry conviction to their minds. They shall not be taught that merit can exist in doing,

The Institution for the Formation of Character

or that demerit can arise from not doing that over which they have no control. They shall not be told, as at present, that they must love that which, by the constitution of their nature, they are compelled to dislike. They shall not be trained in wild imaginary notions, that inevitably make them despise and hate all mankind out of the little narrow circle in which they exist, and then be told that they must heartily and sincerely love all their fellow men. No, my friends, that system which shall make its way into the heart of every man, is founded upon principles which have not the slightest resemblance to any of those I have alluded to. On the contrary, it is directly opposed to them; and the effects it will produce in practice will differ as much from the practice which history records, and from that which we see around us, as hypocrisy, hatred, envy, revenge, wars, poverty, injustice, oppression, and all their consequent misery, differ from that genuine charity and sincere kindness of which we perpetually hear, but which we have never seen, and which, under the existing systems, we never can see.

That charity and that kindness admit of no exception. They extend to every child of man, however he may have been taught, however he may have been trained. They consider not what country gave him birth, what may be his complexion, what his habits or his sentiments. Genuine charity and true kindness instruct, that whatever these may be, should they prove the very reverse of what we have been taught to think right and best, our conduct towards him, our sentiments with respect to him, should undergo no change; for, when we shall see things as they really are, we shall know that this our fellow man has undergone the same kind of process and training from infancy which we have experienced;

that he has been as effectually taught to deem his sentiments and actions right, as we have been to imagine ours right and his wrong; when perhaps the only difference is, that we were born in one country, and he in another. If this be not true, then indeed are all our prospects hopeless; then fierce contentions, poverty, and vice, must continue for ever. Fortunately, however, there is now a superabundance of facts to remove all doubt from every mind; and the principles may now be fully developed, which will easily explain the source of all the opinions which now perplex and divide the world; and their source being discovered, mankind may withdraw all those which are false and injurious, and prevent any evil from arising in consequence of the varieties of sentiments, or rather of feelings, which may afterwards remain.

In short, my friends, the New System is founded on principles which will enable mankind to *prevent,* in the rising generation, almost all, if not all of the evils and miseries which we and our forefathers have experienced. A correct knowledge of human nature will be acquired; ignorance will be removed; the angry passions will be prevented from gaining any strength; charity and kindness will universally prevail; poverty will not be known; the interest of each individual will be in strict unison with the interest of every individual in the world. There will not be any counteraction of wishes and desires among men. Temperance and simplicity of manners will be the characteristics of every part of society. The natural defects of the few will be amply compensated by the increased attention and kindness towards them of the many. None will have cause to complain; for each will possess, without injury to another, all that can tend to his comfort, his well-being, and his happiness.—Such

The Institution for the Formation of Character 109

will be the certain consequences of the introduction into practice of that system for which I have been silently preparing the way for upwards of five-and-twenty years.

Still, however, much more preparation is necessary, and must take place, before the whole can be introduced. It is not intended to put it into practice here. The establishment was too far advanced on the old system before I came amongst you, to admit of its introduction, except to a limited extent. All I now purpose doing in this place is, to introduce as many of the advantages of the new system as can be put into practice in connexion with the old: but these advantages will be neither few nor of little amount. I hope, ere long, even under the existing disadvantages, to give you and your children far more solid advantages for your labour, than any persons similarly circumstanced have yet enjoyed at any time or in any part of the world.

Nor is this all. When you and your children shall be in the full possession of all that I am preparing for you, you will acquire superior habits; your minds will gradually expand; you will be enabled to judge accurately of the cause and consequences of my proceedings, and to estimate them at their value. You will then become desirous of living in a more perfect state of society,—a society which will possess within itself the certain means of preventing the existence of any injurious passions, poverty, crime, or misery; in which every individual shall be instructed, and his powers of body and mind directed, by the wisdom derived from the best previous experience, so that neither bad habits nor erroneous sentiments shall be known;—in which age shall receive attention and respect, and in which every injurious distinction shall be avoided,—even variety of opinions shall not create disorder or any unpleasant feeling;—a society in which individuals shall acquire increased health, strength, and intelligence,—in which their labour shall be always advantageously directed,—and in which they will possess every rational enjoyment.

In due time communities shall be formed possessing such characters, and be thrown open to those among you, and to individuals of every class and denomination, whose wretched habits and whose sentiments of folly have not been too deeply impressed to be obliterated or removed, and whose minds can be sufficiently relieved from the pernicious effects of the old system, to permit them to partake of the happiness of the new.

(The communities alluded to shall be more particularly described in a future publication.)

Having delivered this strange discourse, for to many of you it must appear strange indeed, I conceive only one of two conclusions can be drawn by those who have heard it. These are,—that the world to this day has been grossly wrong, and is at this moment in the depth of ignorance;—or, that I am completely in error. The chances then, you will say, are greatly against me. True: but the chances have been equally against every individual who has been enabled to make any discovery whatsoever.

To effect the purposes which I have long silently mediated, my proceedings for years have been so far removed from, or rather so much in opposition to, the common practices of mankind, that not a few have concluded I was insane. Such conjectures were favourable to my purposes, and I did not wish to contradict them. But the question of insanity between the world and myself will now be decided; either they have been rendered greatly insane,—or I am so. You have witnessed my conduct and measures here for sixteen years; and the objects

The Institution for the Formation of Character 111

I have had in progress are so far advanced that you can now comprehend many of them. You, therefore, shall be judges in this case. Insanity is inconsistency. Let us now try the parties by this rule.

From the beginning I firmly proposed to ameliorate your condition, the condition of all those engaged in similar occupations, and, ultimately, the condition of mankind, whose situation appeared to me most deplorable. Say, now, as far as you know, did I not adopt judicious measures to accomplish these purposes?

Have I not calmly, steadily, and patiently proceeded to fill up the outline of the plan which I originally formed to overcome your worst habits and greatest inconveniences, as well as your prejudices? Have not the several parts of this plan, as they were finished, fulfilled most completely the purposes for which they were projected? Are you not at this moment deriving the most substantial benefits from them? Have I in the slightest degree injured any one of you? During the progress of these measures have I not been opposed in the most determined and formidable manner by those whose interests, if they had understood them, would have made them active co-operators? Without any apparent means to resist these attempts, were they not frustrated and overcome, and even the resistance itself rendered available to hasten the execution of all my wishes? In short, have I not been enabled, with one hand, to direct with success the common mercantile concerns of this extensive establishment, and with the other hand to direct measures which now seem more like national than private ones, in order to introduce another system, the effects and success of which shall astonish the profound theologian no less than the most experienced and fortunate politician?—a system which shall train its children of twelve years old to surpass, in true wisdom and knowledge, the boasted acquirements of modern learning, of the sages of antiquity, of the founders of all those systems which hitherto have only confused and distracted the world, and which have been the immediate cause of almost all the miseries we now deplore?

Being witnesses of my measures, you alone are competent to judge of their consistency. Under these circumstances it would be mere hypocrisy in me to say that I do not know what must be your conclusions.

During the long period in which I have been thus silently acting for your benefit and for the benefit of each of my fellow-men,—what has been the conduct of the world?

Having maturely contemplated the past actions of men, as they have been made known to us by history, it became necessary for my purpose that I should become practically acquainted with men as they now are, and acquire from inspection a knowledge of the precise effects produced in the habits and sentiments of each class, by the peculiar circumstances with which the individuals were surrounded. The causes which had previously prepared my mind and disposition for the work,—which had removed so many formidable difficulties in the early part of my progress,—now smoothed the way to the easy attainment of my wishes. By the knowledge of human nature which I had already acquired, I was enabled to dive into the secret recesses of a sufficient number of minds of the various denominations forming British society, to discover the immediate causes of the sentiments of each, and to trace the consequences of the actions that necessarily proceeded from those sentiments. The whole, as though they had been delineated on a map, were laid open to me. Shall I now at this eventful crisis make the

The Institution for the Formation of Character

world known to itself? Or shall this valuable knowledge descend with me to the grave, and you, our fellow-men, and our children's children, through many generations, yet suffer the miseries which the inhabitants of the earth have to this day experienced? These questions, however, need not be asked. My resolutions were taken in early life; and subsequent years have added to their strength and confirmed them. I therefore proceed regardless of individual consequences. I will hold up the mirror to man,—show him, without the intervention of any false medium, what he *is,* and then he will be better prepared to learn what he *may be.* Man is so constituted, that, by the adoption of proper measures in his infancy, and by steadily pursuing them through all the early periods of his life to manhood, he may be taught to think and to act in any manner that is not beyond the acquirement of his faculties: whatever he may have been thus taught to think and to do, he may be effectually made to believe is right and best for all mankind. He may also be taught, (however few may think and act as he does), that all those who differ from him are wrong, and even ought to be punished with death if they will not think and act like him. In short, he may be rendered insane upon every subject which is not founded on, and which does not remain in never-varying consistency with, the facts that surround mankind. It is owing to this peculiarity in the constitution of man, that when he is born he may be taught any of the various dogmas which are known, and be rendered wholly unfit to associate with any of his fellow-men who have been trained in any of the other dogmas. It is owing to this principle that a poor human being duly initiated in the mysteries of Juggernaut, is thereby rendered insane on everything regarding that monster. Or, when instructed in the dogmas of Mahomedanism, he is thus rendered insane on every subject which has reference to Mahomed. I might proceed and state the same of those poor creatures who have been trained in the tenets of Brahma, or Confucius, or in any other of those systems which serve only to destroy the human intellect.

I have no doubt, my friends, you are at present convinced, as thoroughly as conviction can be formed in your minds, that none of you have been subjected to any such process;—that you have been instructed in that which is true;—that is evident, Pagans, Jews, Turks, every one of them, millions upon millions almost without end, are wrong, fundamentally wrong. Nay, you will allow, also, that they are truly as insane as I have stated them to be. But you will add,—"We are right,—we are favoured of Heaven,—we are enlightened, and cannot be deceived." This is the feeling of every one of you at this moment. I need not be told your thoughts. Shall I now pay regard to you or to myself? Shall I be content and rest satisfied with the sufficiency which has fallen to my lot, while you remain in your ignorance and misery? Or shall I sacrifice every private consideration for the benefit of you and our fellow-men? Shall I tell you, and the whole of the civilised world, that, in many respects, none of these have been rendered more insane than yourselves,—than every one of you is at this moment; and that while these maladies remain uncured, you and your posterity cannot but exist in the midst of folly and misery?

What think you now, my friends, is the reason why you believe and act as you do? I will tell you. It is solely and merely because you were born, and have lived, in this period of the world,—in Europe,—in the island of Great Britain,—and more especially in this northern part of it. Without the shadow of a doubt, had every one

The Institution for the Formation of Character 115

of you been born in other times or other places, you might have been the very reverse of that which the present time and place have made you: and, without the possibility of the slightest degree of assent or dissent on your own parts, you might have been at this moment sacrificing yourselves under the wheels of the great idol Juggernaut, or preparing a victim for a cannibal feast. This, upon reflection, will be found to be a truth as certain as that you now hear my voice.

Will you not, then, have charity for the habits and opinions of all men, of even the very worst human beings that your imaginations can conceive? Will you not, then, be sincerely kind to them, and actively endeavour to do them good? Will you not patiently bear with, and commiserate, their defects and infirmities, and consider them as your relatives and friends?

If you will not,—if you cannot do this, and persevere to the end of your days in doing it,—you have not charity; you cannot have religion; you possess not even common justice; you are ignorant of yourselves, and are destitute of every particle of useful and valuable knowledge respecting human nature.

Until you act after this manner, it is impossible that you can ever enjoy full happiness yourselves, or make others happy.

Herein consists the essence of philosophy;—of sound morality;—of true and genuine Christianity, freed from the errors that have been attached to it;—of pure and undefiled religion.

Without the introduction of this knowledge into full and complete practice, there can be no substantial and permanent ameliorations effected in society; and I declare to you, that until all your thoughts and actions are founded on and governed by these principles, your philosophy will be vain,—your morality baseless,—your

Christianity only calculated to mis-lead and deceive the weak and the ignorant,—and your professions of religion but as sounding brass or a tinkling cymbal.

Those, therefore, who with singleness of heart and mind are ardently desirous to benefit their fellow men, will put forth their utmost exertions to bring this just and humane system of conduct forthwith into practice, and to extend the knowledge of its endless advantages to the uttermost parts of the earth;—*for no other principles of action can ever become universal among men!*

Your time now makes it necessary that I should draw to a conclusion, and explain what ought to be the immediate result of what I have stated.

Direct your serious attention to the cause why men think and act as they do. You will then be neither surprised nor displeased on account of their sentiments or their habits. You will then clearly discover why others are displeased with you,—and pity them. As you proceed in these inquiries, you will find that mankind cannot be improved or rendered reasonable by force and contention; that it is absolutely necessary to support the old systems and institutions under which we now live, until another system and another arrangement of society shall be proved by practice to be essentially superior. You will, therefore, still regard it as your duty to pay respect and submission to what is established. For it would be no mark of wisdom to desert an old house, whatever may be its imperfections, until a new one shall be ready to receive you, however superior to the old that new one may be when finished.

Continue to obey the laws under which you live; and although many of them are founded on principles of the grossest ignorance and folly, yet obey them,—until the government of the country (which I have reason to

The Institution for the Formation of Character

believe is in the hands of men well disposed to adopt a system of general improvement,) shall find it practicable to withdraw those laws which are productive of evil, and introduce others of an opposite tendency.

With regard to myself, I have not anything to ask of you, which I have not long experienced. I wish you merely to think that I am ardently engaged in endeavouring to benefit you and your children, and, through you and them, to render to mankind at large great and permanent advantages. I ask not for your gratitude, your love, your respect; for on you these do not depend. Neither do I seek or wish for praise or distinction of any kind; for to these, upon the clearest conviction, I am not entitled, and to me, therefore, they could be of no value. My desire is only to be considered as one of yourselves,—as a cotton spinner going about his daily and necessary avocations.

But for you I have other wishes. On this day a new era opens to our view. Let it then commence by a full and sincere dismissal from your minds of every unpleasant feeling which you may entertain towards each other, or towards any of your fellow men. When you feel these injurious dispositions beginning to arise,—for, as you have been trained and are now circumstanced, they will arise again and again,—instantly call to your recollection how the minds of such individuals have been formed,— whence have originated all their habits and sentiments: your anger will then be appeased; you will calmly investigate the cause of your differences, and you will learn to love them and to do them good. A little perseverance in this simple and easily-acquired practice will rapidly prepare the way for you, and everyone around you, to be truly happy.

3. Robert Owen: Rational Education for the New Moral World

After the initial formulation of his social philosophy between 1812 and 1820, Owen repeated and elaborated his doctrines many times. In The Book of the New Moral World, *Parts I–VII, he summarized his theories. The following passage on education is from Part III.**

The *known* difference between uneducated and educated man, is the difference now existing between the lowest tribes of human beings, who have but the mere animal education, and those portions of our fellow-men whose physical and mental faculties have been the best educated among the most civilized nations of a most irrational and immoral world, the principles of which are based on falsehood. The *unknown* difference between the highly educated of the old world, and those who shall be educated from birth to become rational in their feelings, thoughts, and actions, who acquire a knowledge of facts, and who are placed under circumstances always to speak the truth, and to be deeply imbued with charity for the thoughts, feelings, and conduct, of all other human beings, is a difference far greater than the known difference now existing between

* *The Book of the New Moral World* (London, 1836–1844), Part III, pp. 41–49.

Rational Education for the New Moral World

the worst and the best educated portions of the human race.

The difference between the *known* most inferior of the human race, formed under the mere animal education, and the unknown excellence and superiority to which man may be educated to attain, physically, mentally, morally, and practically, is the difference to be obtained by the influence of external circumstances in forming the character of the human race. Or—to descend to the familiar language of commerce, the ideas and manners of which now pervade so large a portion of our population—it is the difference between the *material* of *humanity,* as exhibited in each individual of the human race, being *manufactured* in the worst, or in the best manner.

Man will remain blind to his interest and opposed to his own happiness, until he shall know how to well-form his offspring, and shall put that knowledge into practice.

Hitherto man has been kept ignorant of humanity; even now he knows not himself. He imagines the material of which he is formed to be what it never was, what it never can become. In consequence, he has remained ignorant of the principles and process by which humanity can be manufactured to become rational in feelings, thoughts, and actions; and nowhere, at any time, in any part of the earth, have external circumstances been formed to rationalize humanity, or to educate man to become at maturity a rational being. Even now there is not any country in the world in which an establishment exists to well-form the human character, physically, mentally, morally, and practically.

Hence the disordered state of men and nations at the present hour, exhibiting in all their conduct not more, at best, than the germs of future reasonable creatures.

The present chaos of society admits not of the means to form a reasonable human being.

The divisions of society into sects, parties, and classes, into different languages and nations, will, as long as they shall be permitted to remain, hold man in the bonds of ignorance, and keep him in the depths of irrationality. They will continue to train generation after generation in mysteries not to be understood—in divisions of feeling and of interests—in all the inferior passions—and in the same conflicts and random conduct that have marked with blood and folly every page of the past history of man.

If the human race shall ever be well educated—if man shall be made a rational creature, this change can be effected only by the nations of the world being induced, through their sufferings, to consent to supersede all the existing external circumstances of human creation, and all the institutions which have emanated from their erroneous imaginary notions respecting their own nature, and from a want of knowledge of what man, when made rational, may do to secure the happiness of man.

To educate man to become a rational creature, a new combination of external circumstances must be created; each circumstance devised to effect an especial good, in promoting the object to be obtained.

It is a vain anticipation to expect a rational being to be formed in any of the existing establishments for education, in this or in any other country. These are now admirably adapted to force humanity to become insane, and to train all individuals to act the parts of fools or knaves, or both, and to oppose their own happiness and the happiness of their fellow-beings, throughout the whole extent of animal life. By this education the germs of reason are destroyed or misdirected—the feelings are

Rational Education for the New Moral World

diverted from their natural channels—and the whole man is, in consequence, made a diseased animal, physically, mentally, and morally, and a being whose language, thoughts, and conduct, are at continual variance, opposing and perplexing each other, until man becomes at maturity the most inconsistent of all living existences, and the most deceptive of all earthly animals.

And this is the result now produced from that material of humanity which contains within itself the germs of every kind of human excellence and of high attainments;—germs which, when they shall be rationally cultivated, will insure high intellectual, healthy, and joyous happiness to each individual, and to every association of men.

Shall this grossly ignorant and irrational condition of humanity continue through other generations? Must man remain for ever the most inconsistent, and, in consequence, the most miserable being upon earth, when, at the same time, he possesses powers within himself, which, when rightly directed, are competent to insure to him the command of the earth, the happiness of himself, and, to a great extent, the means to make happy all that shall remain upon it?

Nature, through the discoveries made in this generation, emphatically says—"No. The irrational period of human existence shall now cease. I have commenced to open my stores of knowledge and of true wisdom to man, to enable the present generation to start into new life, and break the hitherto hard and impenetrable shell of ignorance which has shut out every ray of rational light from their mental vision. They shall now soon perceive, without the shadow of a doubt, the causes of their mental blindness and their consequent physical and mental afflictions; they shall no longer grope in the dark, but shall distinctly see how to work out their own salvation from ignorance and its consequent errors, producing endless sin and misery. By these discoveries I have given man power to create wealth beyond his wants or desires, to *new*-form the character of all coming generations, and materially, as a preliminary, to *re*form the existing generation, in order that wealth, and knowledge, and excellence, may everywhere abound, and that man may at length enjoy the continually progressively increasing happiness, which, from the beginning, he has been formed at this period to attain."

Such is evidently now the language of NATURE.

She thus speaks aloud through her modern discoveries; her political shaking of the nations, and the agitations throughout the earth arising from the rancorous contests of the opposing Priesthoods of the world.

It is by EDUCATION, rightly understood and wisely applied to practice, that this greatest of all changes in the condition of humanity is now to be effected, to regenerate the human race from its gross irrationalities.

But how is THIS EDUCATION to be obtained, seeing that there are now none but external circumstances which are all calculated to force man to become an inconsistent and irrational being?

By one mode only. Not by hastily and with violence destroying these irrational arrangements of the old worn-out ignorant, immoral, and miserable, world; and treating unkindly those whose characters have been, of necessity, formed by and under these lamentable circumstances; but by gradually, peaceably, and with the kindest feelings to all, introducing a new, scientific, and very superior combination of external arrangements, which shall possess the essence of all that is of real use to man in these old random combinations, leaving out all their

Rational Education for the New Moral World

inconsistencies and absurdities, and uniting all that can be applied beneficially of the late discoveries, inventions, and improvements, to form around man, from his birth, those rational and consistent external circumstances, within which, alone, man can ever be made to become a rational and consistent, and therefore an intelligent, good, and happy, being.

These arrangements are in some degree shadowed forth in the plans described in the "Development of the Principles and Plans on which to Establish Self-supporting Home Colonies," published by the Home Colonization Society, at their office, 57, Pall Mall, London, in the year 1841.

But this publication can give but an imperfect notion of the society that will be formed when there shall be a combination of such nuclei of society, near to and aiding each other, making their whole neighbourhood a portion of an earthly paradise, which, from the excellence and happiness which must be produced and reign throughout the district, will be the cause of the rapid extension of such nuclei over this country, and into other nations, until, by their irresistible advantages, they will extend over every part of the earth.

It is not in any of the old schools, or what are called establishments for education, that a rational character can be formed for man. His powers of mind, his capacity for knowledge, his manners, his spirit, and his conduct, must be formed in the great school, academy, college, and university, of actual life, amidst men and things; with whom and with which, to become eminently useful and happy, he must be early familiarized, and never so placed as to feel it necessary, as at present, to unlearn all that he has been uselessly or mischievously taught amidst conventional errors and absurdities.

It is only amidst the actual active operations of society, when, through all life's departments, the infant, child, and youth, shall be surrounded alone by rational beings, possessing charity and kindness, who will assist wisely to instruct, through every step of this progress, that full-formed rational and superior men and women can ever be produced; but by these means they may as certainly be made, as any superior fabrics are now manufactured from superior arrangements and management intended to produce them.

Man ever has been, is, and ever must be, the creature, to a very great extent, of the external circumstances surrounding him. Put him now permanently within inferior and vicious circumstances only, and he must, with certain limited variations, become inferior and vicious. Place him within superior and really good circumstances, and, in like manner, with certain variations, arising from native individuality of character, he must become superior and good.

It is futile to talk about the details of education, until the great outline of external rational circumstances shall be created, in which rational details can be introduced and daily practised. And to educate aright, men and women must first be trained in normal establishments, to acquire the look, language, manners, and conduct, and especially the spirit, requisite to form and train youth to become rational at maturity. These must be taught, before they can teach others, the *cause* of falsehood, in the look, word, and manner of every individual, and how it is to be removed for ever; the cause of ignorance, of poverty, of division, of all uncharitableness, of crime, of all the inferior passions, and of the want of kindness for all of the human race, and the certain mode by which these causes may be removed from human so-

Rational Education for the New Moral World 125

ciety. These teachers of a rising generation, to make them rational, must themselves be previously instructed how to fill the mind of each pupil with pure unadulterated charity and genuine kindness for the human race, overlooking the present endless ignorances and errors of the poor deluded sects, parties, and classes, into which a want of knowledge of humanity or the eternal laws of human nature, has now divided mankind, and thereby made them inveterate enemies to each other, to the lasting injury of each.

These teachers must be taught the hitherto unknown language of truth without disguise, and how to make it the undeviating habit with all their pupils, and to withdraw all motives from each, ever to desire to express a falsehood by look, word, or action. These instructors must acquire an accurate knowledge of the cause of all anger, to perceive its injustice and irrationality, and to enable their pupils, at an early period, to understand this cause and overcome its effects in their daily intercourse with each other. The same with the causes of pride, vanity, and individual conceit, which they will easily be taught to discover are the necessary results of ignorance of human nature, with the deteriorating influences of praise and blame, rewards and punishments, and all the irrational feelings and notions thence produced.

But it may be asked, where are these rational practices to be taught and acquired? Not within the four walls of a bare building, in which formality predominates, and nature is outraged; but in the nursery, play-ground, fields, gardens, work-shops, manufactures, museums, and class-rooms, in which these feelings will pervade teachers and taught, and in which the facts collected from all these sources will be concentrated, explained, discussed, made obvious to all, and shown in their direct application to practice in all the business of life; in order that each male and female, before the age of twelve, may have a distinct knowledge of the outline of human acquirements, and their existing limits; also of the departments of production and distribution of wealth; and not only of the general principles and practices of the means to produce and distribute wealth in the best manner, but of the necessity for both, and *why* it is to be produced and distributed in the manner that will be adopted in the rational state of society, by all its members at the proper period of life, for producing and distributing wealth advantageously for the whole of society. That they will also know the science or manufacture of human character, how their own had been so far formed in principle and practice, and how they should during their future lives assist to well-form the physical, mental, moral, and practical, character of their younger friends and companions, to make them the best and most superior men and women that their natural faculties would admit; that, in addition, they shall have a distinct knowledge, also, of the principles and practices of rational governing, and understand the causes for and the uses of such form of governing.

In short, as soon as the science of forming the human character shall be taught to the instructors, so that they shall truly understand it, and it shall be properly applied by them in practice, from birth, under all the external circumstances which will be arranged for a rational state of existence, the children so treated, taught, and placed, must become well acquainted with the outline, and much of the detail, of the whole affairs of society, know the past history of their fellow-men, the out-

Rational Education for the New Moral World 127

line of natural history, and what they have to do in the progressive scale of creation, to promote their own happiness, the happiness of their race, and the happiness, as far as practicable, of all that have life upon the earth.

And this now apparently extended education will be imperceptibly instilled into the minds and practice of all, without any overstrained physical or mental exertion, but with great and joyous pleasure to the instructors and the taught; and these results will be produced because all will be done *in accordance with nature,* while heretofore and now *all is done in opposition to nature.*

The acquisition of true principles, of real knowledge, of the spirit of charity and love, and of the natural manners thence ensuing, will be a progress of unmixed pleasure, which will lay a solid foundation for health of body and mind, and active happiness through a long life of satisfied existence.

This is the education which can alone fit man to attain a rational state of existence, to know himself and humanity, to acquire useful and valuable knowledge, to be advanced from being the slave of inferior and vicious circumstances, to a condition in which he will comprehend what are inferior and vicious circumstances, and what are superior and virtuous, how to remove the former, and to replace them with the latter, and to enjoy the necessary results of such a change. In fact, this is the education that will elevate man to a permanently rational and superior state of existence.

From that which has been now written, those who have had minds formed to comprehend the difference between that which is and that which is to be, will readily come to the conclusion that hitherto man has not known what education is, and that no establishment now exists or ever has existed to train any portion of the human race to become at maturity rational beings.

It is the education which has been now described which will prepare the world for the long-promised Millennium; with this difference; that the happiness which it will produce in all will continue and increase with the increase of knowledge, as long as the present earth and its elements shall remain undestroyed.

4. Robert Dale Owen: Education at New Lanark

Owen's eldest son, Robert Dale Owen (1801–1877), taught in the schools at New Lanark and was an enthusiastic believer in his father's doctrines. He settled in New Harmony, Indiana, and became an American citizen. The hopes of what could be expected from education in a community were inspired by such experiences as those he described.*

INTRODUCTION

The system of education which has been introduced at New Lanark, differs essentially from any that has been adopted in a similar institution in the United Kingdom, or, probably, in any other part of the world.

Some particulars regarding it, may, therefore, prove interesting, as exhibiting the results produced on the young mind, by combinations, many of them new, and almost all modified by the general principles on which the system is founded.

It may be necessary to premise, that, the experiment which has been here instituted for the purpose of ascertaining the capabilities of the human mind, at a very early period of life, cannot, by any means, be considered

* Robert Dale Owen, *An Outline of the System of Education at New Lanark* (Glasgow, 1824), pp. 5–77.

as a full and complete, but, on the contrary, as merely a partial and imperfect one; and the results thence obtained, however satisfactory, not as those which a system of training, rational and consistent throughout, may be expected to produce, but only as a proof—an encouraging one, it is presumed—of what may be effected even by a distant approximation to it, under the counteraction of numerous prejudices and retarding causes.

The difficulties and disadvantages, incidental to an experiment of this nature, will be most correctly estimated by those, who may have had an opportunity of witnessing the introduction of any new system, however beneficial; and the pertinacity with which old established habits and ideas continue to hold out against apparently self-evident improvements.

Such individuals will give to the following considerations their due weight:

That, as the children lodge with their parents, and remain in school during five hours only, each day, the counteracting influence of an association with persons who have not received a similar education, must be very great, particularly as those persons, whether parents, relations, or elder companions, are such as, from their age and experience, the children generally look up to with respect, and whose habits and manners they are but too apt to adopt implicitly as a model for their own.

That the difficulty was very great in procuring teachers, who, to the requisite fund of knowledge, general and particular, should unite all the various qualifications of habits, and of temper, so essential in a teacher of youth; unaccompanied too with any pedantry, which might prevent him from regarding his pupils in the light of younger friends, or conversing familiarly with them, and entering into their ideas, or even sometimes into their little projects and amusements, or which might disincline him to be himself, when necessary, instructed and directed.

That, as the parents in general avail themselves of the permission which is granted them, to send their children into the manufactory at ten years of age, the education of these children, being thus broken off at the most interesting and important period, generally remains incomplete; for, although the schools are open in the evening for the instruction of those older children who are employed in the works, yet many do not attend regularly, and it is found that those who do, cannot, after ten hours and a half of labour, apply in the same manner, or derive, by any means, the same benefit from that instruction, as the day scholars.

That many of the children, previously to their admission into the schools, had been permitted to acquire bad habits and improper dispositions, an acquisition which is frequently made, to a great extent, before the little creatures have reached the age of two years, and which most parents, under existing circumstances, have neither the knowledge, nor the means, to prevent. And lastly,

That several of the arrangements, necessary to the completion of the system, are yet only in progress, and that many more remain to be introduced.

New Lanark,
Oct. 1823.

AN OUTLINE, &c.

It will be proper, before proceeding to details, to state the general principles by which these schools are regulated.

The children are governed, not by severity, but by kindness; and excited, not by distinctions, but by creating in them a wish to learn what they are to be taught.

All rewards and punishments whatever, except such as Nature herself has provided, and which it is fortunately impossible, under any system, to do away with, are sedulously excluded, as being equally unjust in themselves, and prejudicial in their effects.

Unjust—as, on the one hand loading those individuals with supposed advantages and distinctions, whom Providence, either in the formation of their talents and dispositions, or in the character of their parents and associates, seems already to have favoured; and on the other, as inflicting farther pain on those, whom less fortunate, or less favourable circumstances, have already formed into weak, vicious, or ignorant,—or in other words, into unhappy beings.

And prejudicial—in rendering a strong, bold character, either proud and overbearing, or vindictive and deceitful; or in instilling into the young mind, if more timid and less decided, either an overweening opinion of its own abilities and endowments, or a dispiriting idea of its own incompetency—such an idea as creates a sullen, hopeless despondency, and destroys that elasticity of spirit, from whence many of our best actions proceed, but which is lost as soon as the individual feels himself sunk, mentally or morally, below his companions, disgraced by punishment, and treated with neglect or contempt by those around him.

It may be a question, which of these two motives, reward or punishment, is in its ultimate effects upon the human character, the more prejudicial, and produce the greater unhappiness; the one in generating pride vanity, inordinate ambition, and all their concomitant irrational and injurious feelings and passions, or the

Education at New Lanark

other debasing the character, and destroying the energies of the individual. And, in this view, the advocates for such a system might perhaps with some plausibility support its *justice,* by arguing—"that the apparent advantages and distinctions, bestowed on already favoured individuals, often cause them more unhappiness and dissatisfaction, than all the mortifications and disappointments of their seemingly less fortunate companions; and thus tend to equalize the amount of positive advantages acquired by each." But surely such an argument is but a poor defence of the system. It is only supporting its justice at the expense of its expediency.

We have said, that all rewards and punishments were excluded from these schools, except those which nature herself has established. By *natural* rewards and punishments, we mean the *necessary consequences,* immediate and remote, which result from any action.

If happiness be "our being's end and aim," and if that which promotes the great end of our being be right, and that which has a contrary tendency be wrong,—then have we obtained a simple and intelligible definition of right and wrong. It is this: *"Whatever, in its ultimate consequences, increases the happiness of the community, is right; and whatever, on the other hand, tends to diminish that happiness, is wrong."* A proposition, at once clear in itself, and encouraging in its application; and one which will scarcely be rejected but by those who are unaccustomed to take a comprehensive view of any subject, or whose minds, misled and confused, perhaps, by words without meaning, mistake the *means* for the *end,* and give to those means an importance, which is due to them only in as far as they conduce to the end itself, the great object of all our pursuits, and the secret mainspring of all our actions.

Every action whatever must, on this principle, be followed by its natural reward and punishment; and a clear knowledge and *distinct conviction* of the necessary consequences of any particular line of conduct, is all that is necessary, however sceptical some may be on this point, to direct the child in the way he should go; provided common justice be done to him in regard to the other circumstances, which surround him in infancy and childhood. We must carefully impress on his mind, how intimately connected his *own* happiness is, with that of *the community*. And the task is by no means difficult. Nature, after the first impression, has almost rendered it a sinecure. She will herself confirm the impression, and fix it indelibly on the youthful mind. Her rewards will confer increasing pleasure, and yet create neither pride nor envy. Her punishments will prove ever watchful monitors; but they will neither dispirit nor discourage. Man is a social being. The pleasures resulting from the exercise of sincerity and of kindness, of an obliging, generous disposition, of modesty and of charity, will form, in his mind, such a striking and ever-present contrast to the consequences of hypocrisy and ill-nature, of a disobliging, selfish temper, and of a proud, intemperate, intolerant spirit, that he will be induced to consider the conduct of that individual as little short of insanity, who would hesitate, in any one instance, which course to pursue. He would expect, what appeared to him so self-evident, to be so to every one else; and feeling himself so irresistibly impelled in the course he followed, and deriving from it, daily and hourly, new gratification, he must be at a loss to conceive, what could have blinded the eyes, and perverted the understanding of one who was pursuing, with the greatest difficulty and danger to himself, an opposite course, pregnant with mortification in its progress, and disappointment in its issue; employing all his powers to

Education at New Lanark

increase his own misery, and throwing from him true, genuine happiness, to grasp for the hundredth time, some momentary gratification, if that deserve the name, which he knew by experience would but leave him more dissatisfied and miserable than it found him.

And his surprise would be very natural, if he were not furnished with the clew, which can alone unravel what appears so palpably inconsistent with the first dictates of human nature. That clew would enable him to trace the origin of such inconsistency to the system of education at present pursued, generally speaking, over the world. Artificial rewards and punishments are introduced; and the child's notions of right and wrong are so confused *by the substitution of these, for the natural consequences resulting from his conduct,*—his mind is, in most cases, so thoroughly imbued with the uncharitable notion, that whatever he has been taught to consider wrong, deserves immediate punishment; and that he himself is treated unjustly, unless rewarded for what he believes to be right;—that it were next to a miracle, if his mind did not become more or less irrational: or if he chose a course, which, otherwise, would have appeared too self-evidently beneficial to be rejected.

The principles that regulate the instruction at New Lanark, preclude any such ideas. A child who acts improperly, is not considered an object of *blame,* but of *pity.* His instructors are aware, that a practical knowledge of the effects of his conduct is all that is required, in order to induce him to change it. And this knowledge they endeavour to give him. They show him the intimate, inseparable, and immediate connection of his own happiness, with that of those around him; a principle which, to an unbiased mind, requires only a fair statement to make it evident; and the practical observance of which, confers too much pleasure to be abandoned for a less generous or more selfish course.

In cases where admonition is necessary, it is given in the spirit of kindness and of charity, as from the more experienced, to the less experienced. The former, having been taught wherein true self-interest consists, are aware, that had the individual who has just been acting improperly, had the knowledge and the power given him, to form his character, he would, *to a certainty*, have excluded from its composition such feelings, as those in which his offence originated; because that knowledge would have informed him, that these were only calculated to diminish his own happiness. The presence of those feelings would constitute the surest proof, that the knowledge and the power had been denied him.

Such, at least, would be the inference we should deduce from similar conduct, in any parallel case. Let us suppose a traveller anxious to reach the end of his journey. He is young and inexperienced, and perfectly unacquainted with the country through which he is to pass. Two roads are before him: the one is smooth and pleasant, affording, at every turn, some new and animating prospect; it leads directly to his object; if he follow it, he will every where meet with agreeable and intelligent companions, all travelling in the same direction, and all anxious to give him every information and assistance. The other, though at first not uninviting, soon becomes dangerous and rugged, leading through a bleak, waste country, the prospect on every side dismal and discouraging; he who pursues it will be continually beset by thieves and assassins; he must be prepared, in every individual he meets, to discover a rival or an enemy; all his fellow-travellers will conceive it to be their

Education at New Lanark

interest to mislead and perplex him; for they know that the inns are few, and small and ill supplied, and that every additional companion lessens the chance of adequate accommodation for themselves: this road, too, dangerous and difficult and disagreeable as it is, gradually changes its direction; it will lead the unfortunate traveller, if indeed he survive its perils and hardships, farther and farther from the object of his destination, and will at last probably conduct him into a strange, barbarous country, where he will sit down in despair, fatigued and harassed, dissatisfied with himself, displeased with his fellow-creatures, disgusted with his journey, and equally afraid and unwilling either to proceed, or to return.

Our traveller, however, chooses this latter path in preference to the other. Now, can we suppose it a possible case, that, at the time he did so, he knew what he was choosing. It is admitted that he *had* a choice, and that he chose evil, and rejected good. But should we therefore assume that he *himself created the preference which gave rise to that choice;* that he *wilfully formed an erroneous judgment;* and that he merited pain and punishment by such perversity? Should we not rather conclude, either that he had decided at random, unconscious of the importance of his choice, or had been deceived by a casual review of the general appearance of the country? Could we avoid remarking, that circumstances which he had not created, and which he could neither alter nor regulate, induced a preference, and thus determined his choice? And if we attempted to put him into the right path, would our language be that of anger or violence? Should we consider it necessary to employ any *artificial* inducements in urging him to change his course? or should we not rather conclude, that this would only lead him to suspect our disinterestedness, and confirm him in the resolution he had already adopted? Nay, if, to ensure his safety and comfort, we proceeded to actual force, and obliged him to take the other path, is it not but too probable, that, as soon as he was relieved of our troublesome presence, he would strike into the first cross-road that presented itself, to return to his original course? How much more easily would the proposed end be effected by a simple dispassionate statement of facts, unaccompanied by violence, and unattended by any artificial inducement! How much more wise would be our conduct if we endeavoured to procure a map of the country, and to prove to the traveller the accuracy of the information we gave; or if we advised him to enquire of those who might be returning from the road he had been so anxious to follow, whether *they* had found it a pleasant or a direct one. They would at once tell him the real state of the case. We might then endeavour to induce him to accompany us in the other direction, only requiring of him that he should look, and hear, and judge for himself.

Now, I believe it to be impossible, that, with even a moderate knowledge of human nature, we should not be able to prove to this traveller, young and inexperienced, and uninformed as he is, our sincerity in the advice we had given him; and I am equally certain, that if we did so, and he believed our statement, he *could* not *deliberately make himself miserable, in preference to making himself happy;* otherwise the desire of happiness cannot be a universal law of our nature.

In the case just stated, the traveller is supposed to commence his journey alone. If he were accompanied by many companions of his own age, and if they all struck into the opposite road, we admit it to be possible that

Education at New Lanark

advice and even conviction might be inefficient to prevent him from going along with them. Man is gregarious; and he might choose to traverse a desert in the company of others, though it led to danger and to death, in preference to beginning a *solitary* journey, though it conducted through gardens to a paradise. But, on the other hand, if his companions followed the road to happiness, it would scarcely be necessary to warn *him* of the danger of separating from them and choosing the other path. If, indeed, *example* and *advice* proved equally unavailing in inducing him to accept of happiness, then nothing less than insanity would account for his conduct; and even in such a case, violence or artificial inducements would prove ineffectual.

We might safely build on a rock, and yet we prefer a bank of sand, artificially supported on all sides, with infinite trouble and anxiety and expense, and which, in all likelihood, the first flood will carry along with it!

Let us suppose a set of children, overawed by the fear of punishment, and stimulated by the hope of reward, kept, which is but seldom the case, during the presence of their teachers in what is called "trim order," apparently all diligence and submission; will these children, we ask, when the teacher's back is turned, and this artificial stimulus ceases to operate, continue to exhibit the same appearance? or are they not much more likely to glory in an opportunity of running into the opposite extreme, and thereby exonerating themselves of a restraint so irksome? Nay, more: impressed as they are with the idea that pleasure and duty run counter to each other, and that, therefore, rewards and punishments are employed to induce them to follow duty at the expense of pleasure, can we expect that such individuals should in after life hesitate to reap present gratification from any line of conduct, not immediately followed by artificial punishment? for that is a *criterion of right and wrong,* which had been brought home to their feelings in too forcible a manner to be quickly forgotten, or easily effaced. Can we wonder that so few individuals leave our schools with other impressions than these? If we do, we surely forget that the law of cause and effect applies equally in the formation of the human character, as in that of a blade of grass or any other natural production.

It is scarcely necessary to allude to the difference which will be found in the character of those, who have never felt these artificial excitements, and whose *youthful* actions have been regulated by a principle, which will operate equally *in after life. They* will know that virtue always conducts to happiness, and that vice leads only to misery; and therefore, they will follow virtue from its own excellence, and avoid vice from its own deformity.

Obstinacy and wilfulness are often fostered, even in generous minds, by a feeling of independence, in rejecting what is attempted to be forced upon them. And public opinion confirms this feeling. He obtains, among his school-fellows, the character of a brave, spirited fellow, who will set himself—whether right or wrong—against the will of their mutual tyrant, for that is the light in which they are too often obliged to regard their instructors. In an institution, conducted on correct principles, the scene is reversed. No credit is obtained, where no risk is incurred. Public opinion is against those who refuse obedience to, or elude commands, which, it is known, are never given but on a reasonable occasion, or enforced, but in a mild and gentle manner. *Obedience* is never confounded with *cowardice,* and therefore obedi-

Education at New Lanark

ence is popular. The most generous and intelligent individuals uniformly lead their companions, and these are gained, when they see themselves treated in a generous and intelligent manner. No party is formed against the authority of the teachers; for even a schoolboy's generosity will not oppose force to mildness, or determined obstinacy to uniform kindness. The teachers are loved, not feared, yet without any deduction from their authority, whenever they find it necessary to exert it. Their pupils converse with them out of school hours, or even during the lessons, when it can be done with propriety, with the most perfect ease and freedom, and such conversation is regarded as a privilege. In the New Lanark institution, this practice has already led to questions and remarks from the children themselves, which would be considered far above their years, and than which nothing can be a greater proof of the good effects of this system of instruction.

What the children have to learn, is conveyed to them in as pleasant and agreeable a manner as can be devised. The subject is selected, and treated with a view to interest them as much as possible. In the lectures, to which we shall presently have occasion to allude, if the interest or attention is observed to flag, the teacher looks to *the lecture itself*, and to his *manner of delivering it*, rather than *to the children*, to discover the cause. It is on this principle, that sensible signs and conversation are made the medium of instruction, whenever it is practicable; and this plan, dictated by nature, has been found to be eminently useful.

Their attention is never confined too long to one object: a lesson for the day scholars, in any particular branch, never exceeding three quarters of an hour.

No unnecessary restraint is imposed on the children;

but, on the contrary, every liberty is allowed them, consistently with good order, and attention to the exercise in which they may be engaged.

By a steady adherence to such a system, but little difficulty will be experienced, in mildly enforcing whatever has once been required of the scholars; even in cases where they may perceive neither the immediate nor ultimate benefit of a compliance.

These principles are no plausible, unsupported theory. Even as such, they appear conclusive. In the absence of any direct experiment, their consistency with every thing we see around us, and with the first feelings and dictates of our nature, would give them no inconsiderable weight. But an experiment has been made under every disadvantage,—what has been done in school has been counteracted without,—(for most of the parents, as was to be expected, do not yet comprehend the utility of this mode of instruction, and have continued their system of rewards and punishments); the teachers themselves have discovered the practice of the system but by degrees; it has been attacked and denounced even by those who had been connected with it—has been cramped by imperfect arrangements; and checked by a mixture of the old with the new principles and practices, inseparable from a first trial;—and yet the result, much as it falls short of what, under different circumstances, might have been obtained, has been, in a very high degree, satisfactory. No such result, as far as we are aware, has hitherto been produced in any similar institution; it is a result, too, which is obtained in the most agreeable manner, both for the instructors and the instructed, without repressing a single generous feeling, and without incurring the risk of abandoning the schoolboy to the world, either as a determined violator of law

Education at New Lanark

and of principle, or as a mean, undecided, dispirited character, equally afraid to do wrong, and unwilling to do right.

Having thus adverted to the general principles by which these schools are governed, the full discussion of which might easily be extended to volumes, and is consequently foreign to our present purpose, we proceed to lay before the public an outline of the details of the plan.

The "New Institution," or School, which is open for the instruction of the children and young people connected with the establishment, to the number of about 600,* consists of two stories. The upper story, which is furnished with a double range of windows, one above the other, all round, is divided into two apartments; one, which is the principal school-room, fitted up with desks and forms, on the Lancasterian plan, having a free passage down the centre of the room, is about 90 feet long, 40 feet broad, and 20 feet high. It is surrounded, except at one end, where a pulpit stands, with galleries, which are convenient, when this room is used, as it frequently is, either as a lecture room or place of worship.

The other apartment, on the second floor, is of the same width and height as that just mentioned, but only 49 feet long. The walls are hung round with representations of the most striking zoological and mineralogical specimens; including quadrupeds, birds, fishes, reptiles, insects, shells, minerals, &c. At one end there is a gallery, adapted for the purpose of an orchestra, and at

* Of these about 300 are day scholars, under ten years of age. The rest are above that age, and attend in the evening when their work is completed; in summer, however, their number is considerably below that here stated.

the other are hung very large representations of the two hemispheres; each separate country, as well as the various seas, islands, &c. being differently coloured, but without any names attached to them. This room is used as a lecture and ball-room, and it is here, that the dancing and singing lessons are daily given. It is likewise occasionally used as a reading room for some of the classes.

The lower story is divided into three apartments, of nearly equal dimensions, 12 feet high, and supported by hollow iron pillars, serving, at the same time, as conductors, in winter, for heated air, which issues through the floor of the upper story, and by which means the whole building may, with ease, be kept at any required temperature. It is in these three apartments that the younger classes are taught reading, natural history, and geography.

We may here remark, that it is probable, the facility of teaching the older classes particularly, would have been greatly increased, had some part of the building been divided into smaller apartments, appropriating one to each class of from twenty to thirty children, provided such an arrangement had not encroached either on the lecture room, or principal school-room.

Each of the two elder classes for the boys, and the same for the girls, who at that age are taught reading, writing, &c. separately from the boys, and only meet them during the lectures, and in the lessons in singing and dancing, consists of from twenty to forty children. The younger classes, composed indiscriminately of boys and girls, are rather more numerous. A master is appointed to each class. There are likewise, attached to the institution, a master who teaches dancing and singing, a drilling master, and a sewing mistress.

At present the older classes are taught reading, writ-

Education at New Lanark 145

ing, &c. in different parts of the principal school-room, the size of which prevents any confusion from such an arrangement; but, as was before observed, the facility with which their attention could be gained, would probably be greatly increased, could a separate apartment be appropriated to each class. The very size of the room, too, increases the difficulty, of itself no slight one, of modulating the voice in reading.

The hours of attendance, in the day school, are from half past seven till nine, from ten till twelve, and from three till five in the afternoon. In winter, however, instead of coming to school again in the afternoon from three to five, the children remain, with an interval of half an hour, from ten till two o'clock, when they are dismissed for the day; making the same number of hours in summer and in winter.

The ages of the children are from eighteen months to ten or sometimes twelve years. They are allowed to remain at school as long as their parents will consent to their doing so; though the latter generally avail themselves of the permission which is granted them, to send their children into the manufactory at ten years of age, or soon after. It is the wish of the founder of these schools, that the parents should not require their children to attend a stated employment till they are at least twelve years old; and it cannot admit of a doubt, that the general adoption of such a measure would be productive of the most important advantages to the parents themselves, to the children, and to society at large.

The infant classes, from two to five years, remain in school only one half of the time mentioned as the regular hours of attendance for the other classes. During the remainder of the time, they are allowed to amuse themselves at perfect freedom, in a large paved area in front of the Institution, under the charge of a young woman, who finds less difficulty—and without harshness or punishment—in taking charge of, and rendering contented and happy, one hundred of these little creatures, than most individuals, in a similar situation, experience in conducting a nursery of two or three children. By this means, these infants acquire healthful and hardy habits; and are, at the same time, trained to associate in a kind and friendly manner with their little companions; thus practically learning the pleasure to be derived from such conduct, in opposition to envious bickerings, or ill-natured disputes.

The school is open in the evening to the children and young persons, from 10 to 20 years of age; the system pursued with them is so similar to that adopted in the day school, that in describing the one, we shall give an accurate idea of the other also.

The dress worn by the children in the day school, both boys and girls, is composed of strong white cotton cloth, of the best quality that can be procured. It is formed in the shape of the Roman tunic, and reaches, in the boys' dresses, to the knee, and in those of the girls, to the ankle. These dresses are changed three times a week, that they may be kept perfectly clean and neat.

The parents of the older children pay 3d. a month for their instruction. Nothing is paid for the infant classes, or for the evening scholars. This charge is intended merely to prevent them from regarding the Institution with the feelings connected with a charity school. It does not amount to one-twentieth part of the expenses of the school, which is supported by the proprietors of the establishment.

It has been deemed necessary, in order to meet the wishes of the parents, to commence teaching the chil-

Education at New Lanark

dren the elements of reading, at a very early age; but it is intended that this mode should, ultimately, be superseded, at least until the age of seven or eight, by a regular course of natural history, geography, ancient and modern history, chemistry, astronomy, &c. on the principle, that it is following the plan prescribed by nature, to give a child such particulars as he can easily be made to understand, concerning the *nature and properties* of the different objects around him, before we proceed to teach him the *artificial signs* which have been adopted to represent these objects. It is equally impolitic and irrational, at once to disgust him by a method to him obscure or unintelligible, and consequently tedious and uninteresting, of obtaining that knowledge, which may, in the meantime, be agreeably communicated by conversation, and illustrated by sensible signs; and which may thus, by giving the child a taste for learning, render the attainments of reading and writing really interesting to him, as the means of conferring increased facilities, in acquiring further information.

The following are the branches of instruction at present taught at New Lanark.

READING

Great difficulty has been experienced, in procuring proper school books for the different classes. Those at present in use, are in many respects defective: they are but ill adapted to the capacities of children so young, and are consequently not calculated to interest them sufficiently. An exception to this last observation must however be made in favour of Miss Edgeworth's little works; but even these contain too much of praise and blame, to admit of their being regarded as unexceptionable. From some little volumes of voyages and travels, too, illustrated by plates and maps, and interspersed with amusing and characteristic anecdotes, great assistance has been derived. The elder classes have often only one copy of each work, from which one of their number reads aloud to the others, who are generally questioned, after a few sentences have been read, as to the substance of what they have just heard. In their answers, they are not confined to the author's words; on the contrary, their answering in a familiar manner, and employing such expressions, as they themselves best understand, is considered as a proof, that they have attended more to the sense, than to the sound.

The general principle, that children should never be directed to read what they cannot understand, has been found to be of the greatest use. The invaluable habit of endeavouring to understand what is read or heard is thus formed. That great and general error, the mistaking of the *means* for the *end*, is avoided, and the erroneous idea excluded, that acquiring a knowledge of the *medium*, through which instruction may be conveyed, is the acquisition of the instruction itself. The children, therefore, after having become acquainted with that medium, will not rest satisfied with this mere mechanical attainment. A knowledge of reading and writing is considered but as furnishing a child with tools, which may be employed for the most useful, or most pernicious purposes, or which may be rusty and unemployed in the possession of him, who having obtained them at great trouble and expense, is yet unacquainted with their real use. The listlessness and indifference so generally complained of by him, whose unpleasant duty it becomes, to force learned, but to them unmeaning sounds, upon his ill-fated pupils, who are thinking of nothing all the time, but the minute that is

Education at New Lanark

to free them from the weary task,—are scarcely known under such a system.*

It is for this reason, that, but for the wishes of the parents, and of parties connected with the establishment, the Scriptures and Church Catechism would not be put into the hands of children, at so early an age as that of the day scholars. There are many parts of the Scriptures, which children of that age should not be made acquainted with, and many more which they cannot understand; and the Catechism of the Scotch Church is so abstruse and doctrinal, that even their superiors in age and understanding might be puzzled, if called upon to explain, what, as children, they learned to repeat.

The children are taught to read according to the sense, and, as nearly as possible, as they would speak; so as, at once, to show, that they comprehend what they are reading, and to give their companions an opportunity of comprehending it likewise. In order to teach them the proper tone and modulation of the voice, the master frequently reads to his class some interesting work; he then allows his pupils to ask any questions, or make any remarks, that may occur to them.

Writing

The mode of teaching writing, is, in the commencement, nearly the same as that adopted in most schools; but as soon as the children can write a tolerably fair text copy, the master begins to teach them current hand writing, according to a plan which has been lately adopted in

* That the system *actually in practice* at New Lanark is imperfect, and consequently incapable of uniformly producing all the results, which would otherwise be obtained—has already been stated.

various seminaries. By this method the children write without lines; and with a little attention, soon learn to correct the stiff formal school hand, generally written, into a fair, legible business hand, such as shall be useful to them in after life.

The writing copies consist of short sentences, generally illustrative of some subject connected with history or geography; and the pupils finally proceed to copy from dictation, or from a book or manuscript, any passage that may be considered as difficult, and at the same time important to be retained in their memory. Thus, as soon as possible, applying the newly acquired medium of instruction in the most efficacious manner.

Arithmetic

Has hitherto been taught on the system which commonly prevails in Scotland. The elder classes, however, are just beginning a regular course of mental arithmetic, similar to that adapted by M. Pestalozzi of Iverdun in Switzerland. In this, as in every other department of instruction, the pupils are taught to *understand* what they are doing; the teacher explains to them *why* the different operations, if performed as directed, must be correct; and in what way the knowledge they are acquiring, may be beneficially employed in after life.

Sewing

All the girls, except those in the two youngest classes, are taught sewing, including knitting, marking, cutting out, &c. One day of the week is appointed, when they are desired to bring to school any of their garments (which must previously have been washed) that may require mending, and these they are taught to repair as neatly as possible.

Education at New Lanark

NATURAL HISTORY, GEOGRAPHY, AND ANCIENT AND MODERN HISTORY

These studies are classed together, because, though distinct in themselves, and embracing, each of them, so great a fund of information, they are taught at New Lanark nearly in the same manner; that is to say, in familiar lectures, delivered extempore, by the teachers. These lectures are given in classes of from 40 to 50. The children are subsequently examined regarding what they have heard; by which means the teacher has an opportunity of ascertaining, whether each individual pupil be in possession of the most important part of the lecture which he has attended. In these lectures, material assistance is derived from the use of sensible signs, adapted to the subject, and which we shall explain more particularly in their place. Each master selects a particular branch, and delivers, as has been already stated, a short lecture to 40 or 50 children at once. The number was formerly from 120 to 150 in one class; but this was found much too large, and one half or one third of that number is as many as it is found expedient to assemble together, except when the lecture is so interesting, as at once to rivet every child's attention, and so easily understood, as to require no subsequent explanation whatever. The attainment of this very important point, it may be observed, will require great attention, considerable ability, and a correct knowledge of human nature. It is extremely difficult for the teacher, particularly if he has had but little experience in delivering lectures to children, to preserve the proper medium between too much and too little detail—to distinguish between unnecessary particulars, which will only divert the attention from the main subject, and those, which are absolutely necessary to children, in the way of explanation. By the former, we refer to such particulars as relate to abstruse questions, to politics, to uninteresting, tedious descriptions of particular animals or countries, especially if these differ but slightly from each other; to any thing, in short, that is not striking and interesting in itself, or becomes so, as illustrative of some general principle, or characteristic of some leading feature. To the latter will belong such simple and distinct details, as may explain the phenomena of nature, of science, or of civilization, together with such as tend to create enlarged ideas, to repress illiberal or uncharitable sentiments on any subject, or to teach children to value every thing for its real worth, and prevent their being misled by the relation of events, which are too often held up as glorious and praiseworthy, but which, reason teaches us, are equally irrational and injurious to the happiness of the community.

In commencing the exposition of any subject, too great pains cannot be taken to avoid all minor details, and, first of all, to give the pupils a distinct outline of what is to be taught them; and to impress this so clearly and definitely on their minds, that they shall be enabled to arrange any subsequent details accordingly. This outline should then be only partially filled up, selecting the most important features, and illustrating these by characteristic anecdotes at greater or less length; than which nothing impresses more distinctly or durably on the mind of a child, the subject to which such anecdote may relate. Subsequently, when further advanced, the pupils may be safely allowed, without fear of perplexing, or overloading their minds, to enter into any important details; and these they will be able at once to classify and appreciate.

These are the general principles, which regulate the

Education at New Lanark

instruction which is given on such subjects, at New Lanark. We are aware how difficult it frequently proves, to deduce from general principles, their practical application; but this difficulty, in the present case, experience will gradually remove.

Natural History is taught to all the scholars, even to the youngest, or infant classes; who can understand and become interested in a few simple particulars regarding such domestic animals as come under their own observation, if these are communicated in a sufficiently familiar manner; for this, indeed, is almost the first knowledge which Nature directs an infant to acquire.

In commencing a course of Natural History, the division of Nature into the Animal, Vegetable, and Mineral Kingdoms, is first explained to them, and in a very short time they learn at once to distinguish to which of these any object which may be presented to them, belongs.*
The teacher then proceeds to details of the most interesting objects furnished by each of these kingdoms, including descriptions of quadrupeds, birds, fishes, reptiles, and insects—and of the most interesting botanical and mineralogical specimens. These details are illustrated by representations of the objects, drawn on a large scale, and as correctly as possible. It is desirable, that these representations should be all on the same scale; otherwise the child's idea of their relative size

---

* Even in the course of such simple illustrations, considerable powers of mind may be elicited. In one of the younger classes at New Lanark, to which the teacher had been explaining this division, the pupils were asked to which kingdom the plaster with which the ceiling of the room was covered, belonged. They answered, "To the Mineral Kingdom;" but one little fellow added, "and to the Animal Kingdom too." And on being asked why? he replied, "Because there is hair in it, and that once belonged to an animal."

becomes incorrect. These drawings may be either hung round the room, or painted, as the botanical representations at New Lanark are, on glazed canvas, which is rolled from one cylinder to another, both cylinders being fixed on an upright frame, at about six or eight feet distance from each other, so as to show only that length of canvas at once. These cylinders are turned by means of a handle, which may be applied to the one, or to the other, as the canvas is to be rolled up or down.

The classes are subsequently, individually, encouraged to repeat what they have heard, to express their opinions on it freely, and to ask any explanation. Such examinations enable the teacher to ascertain, what parts of the lecture have been most suited to the capacities, or calculated to call forth the attention, of the children; and, on the contrary, what portions were too abstruse and uninteresting to be retained. He is thus daily directed in his choice of materials for future lectures; and he gradually discovers the extent of the powers of mind which his pupils possess.

In commencing a course of Geography, the children are taught the form of the earth, its general divisions into Land and Water, the subdivisions of the land into four Continents, and into larger and smaller Islands, that of the water into Oceans, Seas, Lakes, &c.; then the names of the principal countries, and of their capitals, together with the most striking particulars concerning their external appearance, natural curiosities, manners and customs, &c. &c. The different countries are compared with our own, and with each other.

The minds of the children are thus opened, and they are prevented from contracting narrow, exclusive notions, which might lead them to regard those only as proper objects of sympathy and interest, who may live

Education at New Lanark 155

in the same country with themselves—or to consider that alone as right, which they have been accustomed to see— or to suppose those habits and those opinions to be the standard of truth and of perfection, which the circumstances of their birth and education have rendered their own. In this manner are the circumstances, which induce national peculiarities and national vices, exhibited to them; and the question will naturally arise in their minds: "Is it not highly probable that we ourselves, had we lived in such a country, should have escaped neither its peculiarities, nor its vices—that we should have adopted the notions and prejudices there prevalent? in fact is it not evident, that we might have been Cannibals or Hindoos, just as the circumstance of our birth should have placed us, in Hindoostan, where the killing of an animal becomes a heinous crime; or amongst some savage tribe, where to torture a fellow creature, and to feast on his dead body, is accounted a glorious action?" A child who has once felt what the true answer to such a question must be, cannot remain uncharitable or intolerant.

The children acquire a knowledge of the zones, and other artificial divisions of the earth; and it is explained to them, that these are not actual and necessary, but merely imaginary and arbitrary divisions, and that they might have been very different, without in any way altering the real and natural divisions of our globe.

Any one of the older classes at New Lanark, on being told the latitude and longitude of a place, can at once point it out; can say in what zone it is situated, and whether therefore, from its situation, it is a hot or a cold country—what is the number of degrees of latitude and longitude between it, and any other given country, even though on the opposite hemisphere; together, probably, with other details regarding the country; as for instance, whether it is fertile, or a desert; what is the colour and general character, and what the religion of its inhabitants; what animals are found there; when, and by whom it was discovered; what is the shortest way from England to that country; what is the name of the capital city, and of the principal mountains and rivers; and perhaps relate something of its history, or a variety of characteristic anecdotes which he may have heard regarding it. They can thus travel, as it were, over the whole world, taking all the principal countries in rotation.

In the course of the lectures, numerous opportunities present themselves to communicate much general information, not strictly connected with the branches themselves; as for example, descriptions of natural phenomena, of trades, manufactures, &c. Thus, in short, furnishing them with whatever is useful or pleasant, or interesting for them to know.

Ancient and Modern History constitutes another branch of their education. It may be thought, that in teaching History, the aid of sensible signs can be but seldom called in. The reverse, however, is the case. Their application here is, in fact, more complete than in any other branch. Seven large maps or tables, laid out on the principle of the Stream of Time, and which were originally purchased from Miss Whitwell, a lady who formerly conducted a respectable seminary in London— are hung round a spacious room. These, being made of canvas, may be rolled up at pleasure. On the Streams, each of which is differently coloured, and represents a nation, are painted the principal events which occur in the history of those nations. Each century is closed by a horizontal line, drawn across the map. By means of these maps, the children are taught the outlines of Ancient and Modern History, with ease to themselves, and without being liable to confound different events, or different nations. On hearing of any two events, for instance, the child has but to recollect the situation, on the tables, of the paintings, by which these are represented, in order to be furnished at once with their chronological relation to each other. If the events are contemporary, he will instantly perceive it. When the formation and subdivisions of large empires are represented, the eye seizes the whole at once; for wherever the coloured stream of one nation extends over another, on these tables, it is indicative, either of the subjection of one of them, or of their union; and their subsequent separation would be expressed by the two streams diverging again. The children can therefore point out the different historical events, as they do the countries on the map of the world, count the years and centuries as they do the degrees of latitude and longitude; and acquire an idea almost as clear and tangible of the history of the world, as that which the first terrestrial globe they may have seen, gave them of its form and divisions. We know, ourselves, how easily we can call to mind any events, representations of which we were, as children, accustomed to see, and we may thence estimate the tenacity with which such early impressions are retained.

The intimate connexion between Natural History, Geography, and History, is evident, so that in lecturing on one of these subjects, the teacher finds many opportunities of recalling to the minds of his pupils various portions of the others.

Religion

The founder of the schools at New Lanark has been accused of bringing up the children without religion.

The direct and obvious tendency of the whole system of education there, most fully warrants, as it appears to us, a representation the very reverse of this; and as much has been asserted, and still more insinuated on the subject, we may be allowed to state our reasons for this opinion.

An acquaintance with the works of the Deity, such as these children acquire, must lay the basis of true religion. The uniform consistency of such evidence, all nations, and all sects, at once acknowledge. No diversity of opinion can exist with regard to it. It is an evidence with which every one who is really anxious that his children should adopt a true religion, must wish them to become acquainted; whether he may have been born in a Christian country, or be a disciple of Mahomet, or a follower of Bramah. Because simple facts can never mislead, or prejudice the mind. They can never support a religion which is false; they must always support one which is true. He who hesitates to receive them as the basis of his religion, tacitly acknowledges its inconsistency. "And where there is inconsistency, there is error." If the subsequent religious instruction, which a child is to receive, be true, then will the instructor derive, in teaching it, the greatest assistance from the store of natural facts, which the child has previously acquired; because true religion must be completely in unison with all facts. If such subsequent instruction be false, then will it certainly become a difficult task to induce a belief in its truth, because a child, whose mind has been thus prepared, will probably soon discover, that it is not in accordance with what he knows to be true; but every one must admit the advantage of such a difficulty. Even supposing a child instructed in true religion, and believing it implicitly, without, however, having acquired that

Education at New Lanark

belief by deducing its truth from known or well accredited facts,—upon what foundation can such a belief be said to rest? The first sceptic he may converse with, will probably excite a doubt of its truth in his mind; and he himself, being unable to defend his opinions, and having no means of reasoning on the subject, may soon become a violent opposer of that religion, which, though true, had yet been taught to him before he had acquired sufficient knowledge to understand its evidence, or was capable of judging of its truth or falsehood.

This reasoning is peculiarly applicable in the case of any religion, the evidence for which is chiefly derived from historical deductions.

In any other study, the inconsistency of expecting the pupils to deduce correct conclusions before the facts upon which the reasoning proceeds, are known to them, would be glaringly evident. Why then lose sight of this consideration upon a subject so important as religion?

If a chemist were anxious that a child should be able to trace and understand some valuable and important deductions, which with great study and much patient investigation, he had derived from certain chemical facts; would he act wisely in insisting that the child should at once commit to memory, and implicitly believe these deductions? Would he act consistently in objecting to a system, which should first teach the pupil the elements of chemistry, should gradually store his mind with chemical facts, and at length, when his judgment had become matured, place before him these important deductions, and allow him to judge for himself, as to their accuracy?

What should we think of a professor of chemistry, who should object to such a plan? Who would join with him in stigmatizing, as an infidel in the great principles of chemistry, or in denouncing as an enemy to the science itself, the man who expressed his conviction, that it was irrational, before the child could know any thing of the *elementary principles* of the science, to insist upon its *ultimate deductions?* Would not the chemist, who expressed a fear, that unless these were received and implicitly believed *in infancy,* they would not be received or believed *at all,* excite, by the expression of such an opinion, a suspicion of their truth or accuracy?

And is religion a less important, or a less abstruse science than chemistry? Is it of minor consequence that no such cause should exist for attaching suspicion to the great truths of religion? Or are religious doctrines more easily understood than chemical deductions? Or are they not, perhaps, like these, founded on facts? If they are not, they stand not on a rock, but on a sandy foundation. If they are—as it is presumed they must be—then is a knowledge of these facts a necessary preliminary to the study of the science of religion.

As such, it is communicated to the children in the schools at New Lanark.

And on this principle it is considered, that a child, at an early age, should become acquainted with facts, instead of being instructed in abstruse doctrinal points. If it often requires all the powers of the most matured human reason to decide on these points, surely we do wrong to present any of them to the minds of children. Such a proceeding only serves to puzzle and perplex them: it creates listless and inattentive habits: in most cases, it gives children a decided dislike to the study itself. They learn to regard religion, and every thing connected with it, as gloomy, tiresome and mystical; fit only for those, who have lost all power or opportunity of enjoying any thing else.

Education at New Lanark

It would be a libel on religion to suppose these to be the natural consequences of teaching it to children. They are only the necessary results of forcing on the young mind, the prevalent ideas on this subject. Under a different system a religion of confidence, and peace, and love, and charity, could produce neither fear, nor disgust; nor could it ever become unattractive, if presented to children in a simple and natural light. But, in teaching it, we must not depart from those principles, which regulate the rest of our instruction. We must not expect, that children should like a study, which does not interest them, or should feel interested in a study, which they do not understand. If we do, we shall infallibly meet with the results, which alone, as experience tells us, such a system is calculated to produce. But let us not designate these, either the natural consequences of teaching religion, or evidences of the original corruption of the human heart.

If we plant a healthy vine-shoot in an excellent soil; but if, at the same time, being unacquainted with the proper mode of cultivating vines, we neglect to water it, and surround it with a variety of shrubs, by way of support, which, instead of answering this purpose, cramp the growth of the plant, exclude the sun from it, and render it weak and barren; let us not be surprised at the unhappy results of our management; or conclude that no vines planted in that ground can ever flourish or bear valuable fruit; neither let us libel the soil, by imputing to it original, irremediable barrenness. Let us rather inquire if our treatment of the plant be such as nature dictates, or as, reasoning from analogy, and from our previous knowledge of agriculture, we are warranted in supposing conducive to its successful culture. Otherwise it should cease to be matter of surprise, if we find vines flourishing luxuriantly even in wild, neglected spots, while, under our care, they go to decay, and become but a nuisance and a vexation.

To speak without a metaphor—it is not only a fact, that true religion requires no artificial supports, but it is likewise certain, that by surrounding it with these, we only exclude the light of reason, and render principles suspected, the truth of which, if they had not been thus hidden, and obscured, would long since have established itself on the most solid basis.

Again—we are told, that the heart of man "is deceitful above all things, and desperately wicked." And it is undeniable, that the present character of mankind is neither a sincere nor a virtuous one. Indeed, perfect sincerity would expose its possessor either to ridicule, to hatred, or to the imputation of insanity. And any general character approaching to real virtue could not exist under the chilling influence of the existing arrangements of society. This we must acknowledge, with however much regret. But we must be careful in regard to the conclusions we deduce from the fact. We must weigh the matter well, before we admit, that human nature is *necessarily* thus corrupt under every system—or utterly abandon the idea, that the most noble and superior sentiments, good faith, sincerity, generosity, independence and fortitude, kind and social, and charitable feelings, are its inherent qualities, which require only the influence of a mild and genial climate, to draw them forth—and adopt in its place the gloomy picture, loaded with disgusting defects, and sordid qualities, which is held up to us as a true representation of our nature, and over which we may brood, till fancy herself either discovers, or creates the resemblance. If it be correct, then may we give up all hope of any great or permanent

Education at New Lanark

improvement in this world, for the prospect before us is dismal and bleak, and discouraging indeed. It matters not that the intelligence and beneficence of the Creator is conspicuous alike in the instinct, which directs the smallest insect in the way he should go, and in the principle, which regulates and upholds thousands of worlds in empty space. It matters not that every inferior being seems fitted for the condition assigned to it, for man himself, it seems, is not. In his formation, an all-wise and omnipotent Creator has failed. Man's prospects of happiness are indeed fair and promising, but his heart has been made inherently depraved, and must always remain so—and that mars and blasts them all. To attempt its improvement would be in fact to oppose the fiat of his Creator, which has stamped deceit and depravity even on the earliest consciousness of infancy.

In inculcating that religion teaches such a doctrine, let us at least confess to ourselves, that it is one, whose direct tendency is, *to discourage all attempts to promote the virtue or the happiness of the world;* and to fill our mind with vague and painful apprehensions for the future; on the ground, that an *all-good* and *all-powerful* Being has formed, or (which is the same thing) has permitted to be formed in the heart of man, a principle, *which must render all such attempts abortive, and all such apprehensions but too well founded.*

Yet this doctrine, and many others of a similar tendency, form part of the religious instruction which is at present given, even to the youngest children. The world is at issue in regard to many of these doctrines; yet they are unhesitatingly presented, in the most uninteresting and dogmatical manner, to the mind of an infant, and *he* is expected to comprehend them. Can we wonder, that such a mode of proceeding should bring religion into disrepute, and that instructions, given with a view to elevate and ennoble the mind, should in their ultimate effects, but leave behind them an idea of a Being, infinitely powerful indeed, but agitated by human passions, any thoughts of whom it is wise to banish from the mind, as only calculated to terrify and distress;—and an uneasy, undefined feeling of mysterious dread, just sufficient to embitter any moments into which thoughts of religion may intrude.

We act unwisely in adopting a system of religious instruction which shall, in any one instance, have been found to produce such a result.

At New Lanark, every opportunity is embraced of inculcating those practical moral principles which religion enjoins; and of storing the minds of the children, with the most important and striking natural facts; but the consideration of any abstruse doctrines is, as far as the religious views of the parents will admit, reserved for an age, when the pupils shall be better fitted to judge for themselves, and to weigh, with an accuracy, which it would be folly to expect from a child, the opposing arguments that are employed to support or to attack disputed points. By this means, the real interests of truth *must necessarily be promoted;* for it is evident that an individual, whose judgment has been thus informed, must be much less likely to reject truth, or to receive error, than it is possible for the unprepared mind of an infant to be.

It appears to us, that if an individual be sincere in his religious profession, whatever peculiar tenets he may hold, he must, on mature consideration, approve of the plan, which is now suggested, as the most certain method of *disseminating his particular opinions* over the world. And simply because each individual believes his own opinions to be true, or he would not entertain them.

Education at New Lanark

If it be admitted that a very large majority of the religions of the world are false—and it is certain, that only one *can* be true—then does the admission furnish an additional argument in favour of this mode of instruction. For it is very unlikely that any false religion would endure such a test; and it is certain, that a religion founded on reason and on truth, must be essentially promoted by it, to the exclusion of all others.

We shall not enter into any arguments in support of the doctrines propounded by Calvin; nor shall we question their truth or accuracy: the discussion is irrelevant to our present purpose; but it appears to us evident to a demonstration, that if these doctrines are true we cannot adopt a more effectual method of inducing the whole world to become Calvinists, than that now recommended. If false, the sooner they are exploded the better.

It is a fair question, whether too little interference in so delicate a subject as that of religion, or too great latitude in religious toleration, can ever exist. That an opposite system has excited the most bitter and violent of all animosities, that it has armed the neighbour against his neighbour, the father against his children, has destroyed the peace and harmony of families and of nations, has deluged the world with blood, and, under the sanction of the most sacred name, countenanced atrocities, during the relation of which we seem to listen to the history, not of men, endowed with reason, but of demons, possessed with an infernal spirit of savage madness—these are facts, which every page of our history must establish. Can we be too tenacious in maintaining a principle, the practical influence of which, is to prevent *the possibility* of their recurrence?

This is the principle that has always regulated the religious instruction, in the New Lanark Schools. An endeavour has been made to rescue human nature from the imputations thrown upon it by the conduct of individuals, actuated by intemperate religious zeal—a conduct, which has often seemed to justify the strongest expressions regarding human deceit and human depravity. At New Lanark these imputations find no support: in pursuing the system adopted there, no cause of complaint has arisen against the natural depravity of our nature. On the contrary, experience seems completely to warrant the opinion, that our nature is a delightful compound, capable, no doubt, of being formed to deceit and to wickedness, but *inherently* imbued neither with the one nor the other—that if fear be excluded as a motive to action, a child will never become deceitful, for it will scarcely have a motive to deceive.—That if a child be taught in a rational manner, it will itself become rational, and thus, even on the most selfish principle avoid wickedness—and that our only legitimate cause for surprise is the consideration, that human nature, as it now exists, is neither so deceitful nor so wicked as the present arrangements of society would seem calculated to make it.

We should apologize for this digression, but that we feel the importance of the subject, and the necessity that those who would improve and re-form the rising generation, should not create to themselves imaginary difficulties, where no real difficulties exist; and that we have seen how much evil may be done, when a teacher first takes it for granted, that his pupils are all depraved and irrational beings, and then treats them as such. The very tone and manner, which such an idea produces, destroys confidence, and creates distrust and dislike. When confidence is lost and dislike excited, the case becomes indeed hopeless; and the teacher, whatever be his talents, will meet with real and increasing difficulties, and daily

Education at New Lanark

discover fresh cause for distrust and vexation. Unjust suspicion first *creates* its object, and then glories in the penetration which *discovered* it. His pupils must consider that they have no character to lose, and are thus deprived of a great inducement to virtue. They will thwart him in all his measures, and deceive and oppose him on every occasion; because children will not act generously, unless they be treated with generosity.

Before concluding this important subject, it may be necessary to say; that no allusion has been made in this place to a fact which has already been stated; viz. that the scriptures are and have always been statedly read, and the catechism regularly taught there—because this has been done, not as being considered the proper method of conveying religious instruction to the minds of young children, but because the parents were believed to wish it; and any encroachment on perfect liberty of conscience, was regarded as the worst species of tyrannical assumption.

Besides the studies already mentioned, the children are instructed in music and dancing; which are found essentially to contribute towards moral refinement, and improvement. When properly conducted, each of these acquirements becomes a pure and natural source of enjoyment; and it is a well authenticated fact, that the best method of making a people virtuous, is to begin by rendering their situation comfortable and happy.

Singing

All the children above five or six years of age are taught singing, sometimes by the ear, sometimes by the notes. They begin by learning the names and sounds of the notes, and by singing the gamut; then proceed to strike the distances, and finally acquire such a knowledge of the elements of the science of music, as they may easily reduce to practice. The musical notes and signs, as well as a variety of musical exercises, are represented on a large scale, on a rolled canvas, similar to that on which we have mentioned, that the botanical specimens are painted. A small selection of simple airs is made, for the school, every three months. The words to these are printed on sheets, one of which is given to each child. Spirited songs, in the bravura style, are found to be much more adapted to children under ten years of age, than more low and pathetic airs; into the spirit of which they seldom seem to enter, while the former are uniformly their favourite songs, particularly any lively national airs with merry words. Almost all the children show more or less taste for music; although of course this appears in one child spontaneously, while in another it requires considerable cultivation.

The vocal performers in the evening school are sometimes joined by the instrumental band, belonging to the village. This recurs in general once a week.

DANCING

Is taught, as a pleasant, healthful, natural and social exercise, calculated to improve the carriage and deportment, and to raise the spirits, and increase the cheerfulness and hilarity of those engaged in it. The dances are varied. Scotch reels, country dances, and quadrilles are danced in succession; and by some of the older pupils with a simple and unaffected ease and elegance, which we have never seen surpassed in children of their age.

Besides dancing, the children, boys and girls, now and then go through a few military evolutions, as well to give them the habit of marching regularly from place to

Education at New Lanark

place, as to improve their carriage and manner of walking. This species of exercise is never continued long at a time; and stiffness and unnecessary restraint are avoided as much as possible; on the principle, already mentioned, and which pervades the whole of the arrangements in these schools, that whatever is likely to prove unpleasant or irksome to the children, and is not necessary for the preservation of good order, or for some other useful purpose, should never be required of them. At the same time, whatever is really necessary to the proper regulation of the school, is uniformly but mildly enforced.

To prevent any confusion or irregularity, each teacher is furnished with a list of the lessons, which his class is to receive during the week, and these are of course so arranged, that the lessons of the different classes cannot interfere with each other.

The general appearance of the children is to a stranger very striking. The leading character of their countenances is a mixed look of openness, confidence and intelligence, such as is scarcely to be met with among children in their situation. Their animal spirits are always excellent. Their manners and deportment towards their teachers and towards strangers, are fearless and unrestrained, yet neither forward, nor disrespectful. Their general health is so good, that the surgeon attached to the village, who is in the habit of examining the day scholars periodically, states, as the result of an examination, which took place a few weeks since; that, out of 300 children, only three had some slight complaint; and that all the others were in perfect health. The individual literary acquirements of the greater proportion of the older classes, are such as perhaps no body of children of the same age, in any situation, have had an opportunity of attaining. The writer of the present article has had frequent opportunities of examining them individually; and he has no hesitation in saying, that their knowledge on some of the subjects, which have been mentioned, as forming part of their instruction, is superior to his own.

A sufficient degree of friendly emulation is excited amongst them, without any artificial stimulus; but it is an emulation, which induces them to prefer *going forward with their companions,* to *leaving them behind.* Their own improvement is not their only source of enjoyment. That of their companions they appear to witness with pleasure, unmixed with any envious feeling whatever; and to be eager to afford them any assistance they may require. Some of them have voluntarily undertaken, when any of their companions were necessarily absent during some interesting lecture, to give them all the particulars they should be able to recollect of it, as soon as they returned home.

Although there have always been schools at New Lanark, and although the building which is at present employed as a school, has been open for eight years, yet several material parts of the system have been in operation scarcely two years—so that their ultimate effects cannot yet be fully ascertained. As far as these have yet appeared, however, they have been most satisfactory. It has always been found, that those children, who made the greatest proficiency in their various studies and acquirements, proved subsequently, the best, the most industrious and most intelligent assistants, both as workpeople and domestics.

There are persons, who will admit the general consistency and excellency of such a system of education, but who will, nevertheless, object to it, as totally un-adapted to the lower or working classes.

That true knowledge uniformly conduces to happiness is a fact, which, though it was denied in the dark ages of the world, is very generally admitted at the present day.

The acquisition of true knowledge, therefore, must increase the happiness of those who acquire it. And if the lower classes have fewer outward sources of enjoyment, than their more wealthy neighbours, then does it become the more necessary and just, that they should be furnished with means of intellectual gratification.

We admit, that the lower classes cannot receive such an education, and yet remain in their present ignorant and degraded state. We admit, that it will make them intelligent and excellent characters. That, when they are placed in a situation which is really improper, it will necessarily make them desirous of changing and improving it. We admit, that the real distance between the lowest and the highest ranks will be decreased. That the ultimate result will be such an improvement of habits, dispositions and general character in those in subordinate situations, as will induce us to regard them in the light of assistants rather than of dependants. We admit, that its general introduction will gradually render all ranks much more liberal, better informed, more accomplished, and more virtuous than the inhabitants of Great Britain are at this moment. And that, in short, its direct tendency will be, to enlighten the world, to raise all classes without lowering any one, and to re-form mankind from the least even to the greatest.

But we misconceive its tendency, and mistake its effects, if we imagine that real, solid intellectual improvement, will ever induce the lower classes to envy the situation, or covet the possessions of the wealthy. Or that it will ever raise any of them above a proper employment, or render them dissatisfied with any state of things, that is really beneficial to themselves or useful to society. Or that it will create seditious principles, or excite revolutionary ideas in their minds. Or, in short, if we suppose that true knowledge will ever conduce to misery. We are in error if we conceive, that it is more pleasant to be surrounded by servile dependants, than by enlightened assistants—or, if we believe, that even the selfish interests of the higher ranks can be promoted by increasing the distance, and thus widening the breach between them and another class of their fellow-creatures —or that the sufferings and degradation of the one class can, in any way, increase the actual enjoyment of the other.

Indeed, the idea, that such a notion is deliberately entertained by the higher classes, presupposes in them a want of feeling, inconsistent alike with every superior sentiment, and with their own real or permanent happiness.

5. Robert Owen: Ten Rules for an Infant School

Owen had a great love for children, and his infinite patience and good temper made him a beloved figure to them everywhere. This summary of his principles for the conduct of the New Lanark schools is from his Life.*

That which I introduced as new in forming the character of the children of the working class may be thus stated—

1st.—No scolding or punishment of the children.

2nd.—Unceasing kindness in tone, look, word, and action, to all the children without exception, by every teacher employed, so as to create a real affection and full confidence between the teachers and the taught.

3rd.—Instruction by the inspection of realities and their qualities, and these explained by familiar conversations between the teachers and the taught, and the latter always allowed to ask their own questions for explanations or additional information.

4th.—These questions to be always answered in a kind and rational manner; and when beyond the teacher's knowledge, which often happened, the want of knowledge on that subject was at once to be fully admitted, so as never to lead the young mind into error.

* Life of Robert Owen, Written by Himself (2 vols.; London, 1857–1858), I, 232–233.

5th.—No regular in-door hours for school; but the teachers to discover when the minds of the taught, or their own minds, commenced to be fatigued by the in-door lesson, and then to change it for out-of-door physical exercise in good weather; or in bad weather for physical exercise under cover, or exercises in music.

6th.—In addition to music, the children of these workpeople were taught and exercised in military discipline, to teach them habits of order, obedience, and exactness, to improve their health and carriage, and to prepare them at the best time, in the best manner, when required, to defend their country at the least expense and trouble to themselves.

They were taught to dance, and to dance well, so as to improve their appearance, manner, and health. I found by experience that for both sexes the military discipline, dancing, and music, properly taught and conducted, were powerful means to form a good, rational, and happy character; and they should form part of the instruction and exercise in every rationally formed and conducted seminary for the formation of character. They form an essential part of the surroundings to give good and superior influences to the infants, children, and youth, as they grow towards maturity.

7th.—But these exercises to be continued no longer then they were useful and could be beneficially enjoyed by the taught. On the first indications of lassitude, to return to their in-door mental lessons, for which their physical exercises had prepared them, and to which, if properly conducted, they will always return with renewed pleasure. And to receive physical or mental exercise and instruction may always be made to be highly gratifying to the children, when they are rationally treated.

Ten Rules for an Infant School 175

8th.—To take the children out to become familiar with the productions of gardens, orchards, fields, and woods, and with the domestic animals and natural history generally, is an essential part of the instruction to be given to the children of the working classes; and this was the practice in my time with the children at New Lanark.

9th.—It was quite new to train the children of the working class to think and act rationally, and to acquire substantial knowledge which might be useful to them through after life.

10th.—It was quite new to place the child of the working man within surroundings superior to those of the children of any class, as was done in a remarkable manner at New Lanark, by placing them during the day in the first and best institution for the formation of the character of the children of workpeople ever thought of or executed.

But it must be yet some time before these new practical proceedings for the children of the producers of wealth can be duly appreciated; or their importance for the advancement and permanent benefit of society can be comprehended.

6. Jane Dale Owen: The Principles of Natural Education

The following lecture was written by Owen's second daughter, Jane Dale Owen (1806–1861), and revised by his eldest daughter, Ann Caroline. Jane settled in New Harmony, Indiana, where she married Robert Fauntleroy.*

Few there are, in the present day, who are not deeply impressed with the importance of Education; yet, in proportion as the notions regarding it have been limited and imperfect, has the interest which it has excited, been less than the subject demands. When we consider that it is a subject in which is involved the happiness and well-being of the whole human race, do we not feel that it calls for the undivided attention of every reflecting mind?

As the ideas upon education have hitherto been limited and imperfect, so the term has been made use of in a narrow signification: I speak of it now in an extended sense—the only sense in which it ought to be understood—as signifying a general superintendence of the individual from birth to maturity; thus including the cultivation of all his powers, physical, mental, and moral, and the placing him under such circumstances as are best suited for the development of his character.

* In Robert Owen, *Lectures on an Entire New State of Society* (London, 1830), pp. 113–122.

The Principles of Natural Education 177

To explain to you the best mode of effecting these objects, or, in other words, to lay down the outlines of a system of education, founded upon the unerring laws of our nature, is the end I have now in view. But, first, it may be useful to enquire, what is the method, under the name of education, now generally pursued, and the results most commonly obtained; proceeding next, to examine the nature of the foundation upon which it rests.

During the first years of infancy, although it is an acknowledged fact that the child at this period is capable of receiving, and, in truth, does receive his strongest impressions, yet, under the present irrational mode of proceeding, the development of his powers is left almost wholly to the guidance of chance, and his mind is subjected to the baneful influence of the caprice of others— generally of those, whose very limited knowledge renders them, least of all, fitted for the task of control. Thus neglected and injured, the child enters upon what, in the present acceptation of the term, is denominated his education. He becomes acquainted with the rudiments of learning, yet scarcely one particle of real knowledge does he possess. He is filled with superstitious notions and fears concerning Deity, yet is left wholly uninformed regarding himself. He is rendered familiar with the languages of ancient Greece and Rome, yet most frequently remains ignorant of the commonest natural facts. And at what price are obtained even these limited acquirements?—At the sacrifice of his moral feelings. He is taught to emulate his fellows; and thus becomes jealous of those superior to him and arrogant to those inferior. I have spoken now of our male youth; yet, with additional force, will the remarks apply to our females. In proportion as their physical powers are less vigorous and their mental susceptibility is greater, are they rendered more feeble in body and more degenerate in mind. Thus do both sexes emerge upon the great scene of life, with powers ill-apportioned to the task which awaits them. They become fathers, mothers; and thus perpetuate the evils of which they themselves have been made the slaves. I ask, my friends, can such a system have, for foundation, aught but principles of a fallacious nature? The tree is known by its fruit. Mischievous results are the consequences of false principles of action; and thus it is with the present mode of education. Parents, guardians, and instructors of youth, enter upon their task with erroneous notions regarding human nature, and the issue is fatal to the happiness and well-being of the objects of their care. They are of opinion, that in human nature, the evil preponderates over the good, or, in other words, they believe in the doctrine of Original Sin. Hence, by looking for evil instead of good, they often view the actions of a child through a false medium; and by mistaking the source whence his errors proceed, apply an unsuitable, and therefore, an unsuccessful remedy. They believe that in him is vested, as well as the power to perform, the free will to choose between good and evil; and, consequently, they praise when his conduct is good, blame him when it is the reverse—confer reward upon him in one case, load him with punishment in the other. Hence the jealousy, hatred, and strife, which take rise among children; and hence the foundation of those evil passions, which shew themselves, with increased violence, in human beings of maturer age.

My friends, experience and reflection have now demonstrated to us, past a doubt, that these two principles, upon which the education of the young is commonly based, are false principles; and that, in fact, those only of a directly opposite tendency are true, and calculated

The Principles of Natural Education 179

to obtain the wished-for results. We believe, not that the child is imbued with evil, but, that he is endowed with qualities of a mixed character, some of them superior, others of an inferior nature; and that, according to the peculiar mode of training adopted, so will the one or the other predominate. And why do we so believe? Because acting under favourable circumstances, we see one individual become a pattern of virtue; placed in unfavourable circumstances, we behold another practising every species of vice. When a seeming contradiction to this takes place, it must arise either from the original conformation being inferior in the one and superior in the other, or, from the treatment applied being unsuited to the character. For a similar reason, as that I have now stated, viz., that the individual is plastic in the hands of those who surround him, we believe not that he is responsible for his actions; and, consequently, is undeserving of praise or of blame, of artificial reward or of punishment. Can the Jew, the Christian, the Mahometan, the Hindoo, or the Pagan, be justly held responsible for his religion, when the faith which he professes is determined by the geographical circumstances of his birth? Can the monarch, or the pauper, the wise man or the ignorant, the virtuous or the vicious, have aught of merit or demerit ascribed to him for the particular character which he possesses, when that character has been communicated to him by the circumstances in which he has been placed? Thus, having plainly no participation in his original conformation, and no choice in determining the peculiar situation in which he shall be placed, we cannot reasonably ascribe to him accountability for his actions. Shrink not at the withdrawal of this fallacious doctrine, although it has, hitherto, been falsely regarded as the shield to virtue: rejoice, rather, that man needs it not. And why? Because it is placed at our disposal to mould him as we will. Shall we not then, by substituting truth for error, and good for evil, henceforth render him virtuous, wise, and happy?

Proceeding upon this broad foundation, I would now, my friends, briefly detail to you the system of education which ought to be raised upon it; a system which, by co-operating with, instead of counteracting nature, would infallibly prove successful.

And first, let me remark the necessity of taking an extended view of man's constitution, and of the order in which his various powers are developed; a duty which, by the guardians of youth, has hitherto been wholly neglected. Thus he primarily exercises his instructive impulses. Next, his moral qualities. Thirdly, his intellectual faculties. In the same order do they call for attention and regulation.

During the earliest years of childhood, when, as I before stated, the impressions are the strongest, let the individual be made to feel and observe, the advantage resulting from moderation in gratifying his instructive impulses; and providing he is denied nothing in that measure, which nature demands, he will, assuredly, thenceforth practice that moderation. Hitherto, no definite measure of this kind has been adopted, and the fatal consequences have been but too apparent.

The cultivation of the moral qualities next demands our attention. And here I would remind you, that education must commence in the very cradle, from the moment in fact in which the infant first awakes to consciousness; for, from that moment he begins to acquire ideas. Our duty then is to guard against his receiving any other than *right* ideas; and in order to effect this, our own actions must be regulated. He ought never to be

The Principles of Natural Education

made the recipient of anger, nor be witness to it; the tone of voice ever expressing to him feelings of the utmost kindness. He ought, as an infant, to be presented with no objects but those which it may be beneficial for him to examine; as his natural curiosity prompting him so to do, he is often, upon refusal led into ebullitions of passion, which gradually become habitual. He should have no deceit practised upon him, nor made a participator by any. Thus guarding, in the earliest period of his existence, against every contingency which may communicate to him evil habits, we shall, when he has attained sufficient age, have a fair field upon which to enter, in the cultivation of his moral qualities. And, my friends, how mightily will the task be lightened. He who has seen no anger, will he be liable to feel resentment? He, who has been witness to no deceit, will he be untruthful?

I describe, however, as you will readily perceive, a mode of education which can be realized only when men shall have adopted a system of society under which they can all act rationally.

Ought we then in justice, ought we longer to delay the establishment of such a system, when upon its introduction depends the happiness and welfare of our posterity?

But to proceed.—As soon as the opening mind of the child shall be able to comprehend abstract truths, a period which, under this superior mode of training, would be considerably hastened, he should, with a view to confirm the habits he had previously acquired, of moderation, mildness, and candour, be made acquainted with the great laws of our nature, and especially of the important one, that man forms not his own character, and consequently is not responsible for his actions. Thus, he would acquire just ideas concerning himself; and thus would there be withdrawn from his mind all motives to anger, revenge, hatred, jealousy, or other malevolent passions. He would next be led to observe the happy consequences resulting to himself and others from a virtuous and amiable mode of conduct, and the evil consequences which would ensue by his pursuing an opposite course; while, until he obtain the requisite experience, every temptation to err, which it is possible to remove, should be withdrawn. So soon as he shall have acquired that experience, and his habits become confirmed, no such guard will be necessary. Can any one, but he who is thoroughly imbued with the idea of man's depravity by nature, refuse to anticipate with me, that a character, modelled by these simple, yet all-powerful means, would inevitably become an amiable and a virtuous character, happy in himself, and communicating happiness to all around him? And, I appeal to you, would a necessity exist for the idea of man's accountability to keep such a character in check? No! furnished with far more enduring principles of action, viz. early habits, and the pleasurable feelings resulting to him from his particular mode of conduct, he would never swerve from the right path.

To what end should nature have instituted the law, that virtuous conduct is invariably followed by satisfaction and pleasure, whether derived from our inward feelings, or the approbation of others, unless to serve as a guard to our virtue, and consequently our happiness? I argue, therefore, such is the only just, and hence, aided by early habit, will prove the only unfailing motive, with which to furnish the young mind.

Having thus pointed out the course to be pursued in the cultivation of the moral qualities, I enter now upon

The Principles of Natural Education 183

an explanation of the best means of developing the intellectual faculties. Again I must refer to the earliest period of childhood, for although the various powers of the individual are developed, and consequently demand peculiar care, in the order in which I have stated them, yet the preparation for the culture of each must commence in the cradle. As soon, therefore, as the child exhibits signs of intelligence, he should, in order to strengthen and develop his faculty of observation (which is the first mental power he exercises), be permitted and encouraged to examine minutely whatever comes under his view, or appears particularly to attract his attention. Thus, a spirit of inquiry being awakened in his mind, and a habit fixed, of keen and accurate observation, he will, during his succeeding years of infancy, be led to acquire, with precision, a knowledge of all facts, particularly in the natural world, which may come within his comprehension; and thus will be opened to him a path leading to the acquisition of more useful information than many, trained under the old system of education, receive during their lives. The habit of accurate observation is one which is particularly important, inasmuch as it assists in the exercise of many of the other mental powers; we cannot then too carefully direct the first operations of this faculty.

Taking nature for our guide, we find the rules to be observed, in the development of the remaining intellectual faculties, to be the following:

1st. Never to demand attention from a child to any subject unsuited to his years or capacity, or to require it from him, on any occasion when it is not spontaneous.

2nd. To tax his memory, for the first years of his life, with such particulars only as are similar to those which he may himself gather from the faculty of observation, that, having a standard to which to refer, he may be able to recall, at pleasure, the ideas at first communicated to him.

3rd. To encourage him to dwell upon each of these ideas separately, and to examine it apart from all others. Thus will be given to him the power of *abstraction*.

4th. To present to his young mind no ideas but those conveying to him a knowledge of facts; facts ascertained to be such, by the test of consistency; hence the foundation of an accurate judgment.

5th. To accustom him early to the practice of comparison and of inference; that, at a maturer age he may be able to draw, with precision, conclusions from previous premises, and to trace effects to their causes. Thus will he be put in possession of a power, which, added to experience, will enable him to ascertain "What is truth?"

6th. To keep the imagination always in subservience to the judgment; and this being observed, to excite the young mind (where such an impulse appears necessary) to form occasionally new combinations of ideas for itself.

7th. To suffer no one faculty to neutralize the other, or, in other words, to develop them all equally.

Such, my friends, is an abstract of the method, which nature teaches us ought to be pursued, in the development of the intellectual faculties. I hesitate not to say, that, except in cases of original incapacity, it is calculated to form a mind of the highest order.

In what degree the system usually adopted accords with that I have now described, I leave my hearers to determine. Lamentably is the truth regarding it forced upon our conviction, by living examples of folly, of imbecility, and of ignorance!

I have hitherto spoken of the cultivation of the mental

The Principles of Natural Education 185

powers: I would now, with scarcely less earnestness, press upon your attention the cultivation of our physical powers, for upon the one does the other depend.

The character of our physical powers is determined by the nature of our food, our clothing, and the degree and kind of exercise we may habitually take. The child then, from early infancy, ought to be subjected to a regular mode of training in these particulars; his food, being that best suited to his constitution, his clothing, that best adapted to the climate; and the exercise he may enter into, that best fitted to improve his peculiar organization.

Generally speaking, the simplest food and the lightest clothing will be found the most healthful, and that variety of exercise the most advantageous which gives to the human frame at once vigour and elasticity. To this end, a regular set of gymnastic exercises, formed upon this principle, ought to be practised by both sexes; and any other facilities afforded them, adapted to each, which may be found necessary. Greatly have we degenerated in physical strength since the days of our forefathers, or those of the ancient Greek and Roman attiletæ. They, however, almost wholly neglected the cultivation of the mind. Let us unite both, and thus secure, for future generations, a higher character, bodily and mentally, than that which any portion of men has hitherto attained.

I would now, in conclusion, shortly advert to the various kinds of knowledge proper to be communicated to the young mind, and the manner in which that knowledge ought to be applied.

Experience has taught us, that the ideas best calculated to inform and to interest the understanding of a child are those which relate to natural facts. It seems, therefore, to be dictated by nature, that such only, for the first years of his present instruction, prepare his mind for the reception, at a future period, of abstract truths. As soon then as he is capable of fully comprehending language, (a period which will vary in each different case,) the child ought to be brought under a regular organized system of instruction in natural knowledge, proceeding from the most obvious and easily understood facts, to those which are more complicated and less apparent.

The *manner* of imparting knowledge is equally important with the *matter,* inasmuch as it determines the success of the teacher. From dry and uninteresting details, clothed in language unsuited to his capacity, the young mind turns away. Hence we learn, that the words employed ought to be simple, and the particulars selected for narration, few and striking. I say narration, for, at this period, all instruction should be oral, accompanied, if possible, by sensible or representative signs of the objects described.

This preparatory system ought to embrace,—General Knowledge relative to the three kingdoms of Nature, Geography, and an acquaintance with the laws of attraction, gravitation, &c., the elements of Chemistry, of Geometry, and of Numbers; all of which are calculated to expand the young mind, and to render its observations accurate.

As soon as the child shall be in possession of the facts included in these, then, and not until then, should he be made acquainted with the symbols of knowledge, viz. reading, writing, and the rules of arithmetic. And for this obvious reason,—that, until he acquire the knowledge of which these are merely the signs, they must convey to him no definite meaning: hence the labour and time now consumed in imparting these to children;

while, by reversing the system, a much less proportion of each would be required.

The period of the child's life, probably to his tenth year, during which the preparatory system I have spoken of should extend, is now generally spent under the guidance of his mother. However endearing the tie, it may be questioned whether she is the fittest person to undertake the task; and, certainly, as the education of females is at present conducted, no one can be less so. Yet, looking forward even to a happier period, the time when knowledge shall be universally diffused, I believe, for two reasons, that the superintendance of the child ought to pass into other hands, or, at least, be shared by the mother with qualified individuals.

First, because affection is apt to warp the judgment; next, because a solitary, or even a family education, is unfavourable to the human being. Schools, then,—public schools, but diametrically opposite in nature and tendency to the public schools of the present day,—ought to be instituted for both sexes. Each of these seminaries, conducted as it would be, upon a system calculated to perfect the moral qualities, and develop the intellectual faculties, would form the cradle of virtue and the nursery of genius. Thus, I apprehend, a similarity between these and the great body of the public schools of the present day could be traced in no other particular than the name.

As the human being approaches to maturity, the plan of tuition ought to be enlarged. Each individual should be made acquainted with the arts and sciences, so far as their practical use extends, and facilities be afforded for deeper research, to those who exhibit a desire or capacity to pursue any one of them in particular. As a study of inestimable value, much attention should be paid to every branch of physiological knowledge, as the individual possessed of this would be enabled to govern himself, bodily and mentally, and be well fitted to discharge his social duties; thus removing the necessity of any one exclusively following the profession of priest, physician or lawyer, a constitution of society which is at once injurious to the individual himself and to the community at large.

The study of mankind having now discovered to us, that manual labour, as affording the requisite degree of exercise, is essential to the health of the physical and mental powers, and, as contributing to supply the wants of society, is an obligation which every individual owes to his fellow-man, a regularly organized system of manual labour ought to be united, in every case, with one of mental and moral culture.

Thus, while each child received health and pleasure, he would earn, in part, his own subsistence, and acquire those habits of industry and independence which are calculated to render him a useful and a happy man.

My friends, I have thus developed to you a system of education, "based on the unerring laws of our nature;" and as such, so far as our knowledge extends, a perfect one. To that enlightened period, when men shall unite to promote the public good, a period which, I trust, is rapidly approaching, do I look for its adoption.

7. Abram Combe: The Definition of Education

The leader of the first Owenite community in Britain was Abram Combe (1785-1827). After his conversion to Owenism he wrote several works explaining the new view of society, and in the following extract defends the Owenite concept of education against criticisms in the Scotsman *newspaper.**

The first step . . . will be to get a clear definition of the term "Education."

To our minds, it conveys the idea of acquiring the arts of reading and writing; and also an acquaintance with the dead and foreign languages, and other branches of polite learning.

An Individual who has been made skilful in these acquirements is generally considered to have got a "Good Education."—In this view, the New System differs completely from the old.—The New System calls Education the *"Acquisition of Ideas;"*—and the ideas which convey correct representations of *Realities,* it calls *"Sound Ideas."*

So that, under the New Views, a plentiful collection of sound ideas is termed, a "Good Education."

---

* See Abram Combe, *Metaphorical Sketches of the Old and New Systems* (Edinburgh, 1823), pp. 97-107. See also p. 8, n. 13.

When a child first sees a Horse, it gets a correct idea of a Horse. If you attempt to give the child an idea of any object by words, the task is not only disagreeable and unprofitable to both parties, but it is absolutely endless.—It is upon this account that the Founder of the New System proposes to introduce sensible signs as the best means of educating children; and when the object itself cannot be introduced, it is supposed that a correct representation of it will best supply the deficiency.

A little reflection will convince us, that the old ideas, on the subject of Education, are extremely absurd; and that the arts of *Reading and Writing,* and an acquaintance with the dead and foreign languages, are merely *the means by which we may acquire an Education.*— Because, by means of these, we may acquire either correct ideas, or those that are incorrect.—All ideas which do not correspond with the realities, are incorrect; and all the ideas that we get solely by means of words, are, without exception, more or less of this description.— We must all have observed, that ideas of the simplest objects in nature, which we had got by *mere description,* never, in one instance, corresponded with the reality. For instance, we cannot enter a town, for the first time, without perceiving a great dissimilarity betwixt it and the idea we had previously formed of it; and it is the same in every other case.

It thus becomes evident, that what we have hitherto called *Education,* is neither more nor less, *than the most deficient means of acquiring an Education,* which, when it is acquired, may be either Good, Bad, or Indifferent.

Education, in a rational sense, means the Ideas, which are impressed on the mind of the individual, by which his Judgment is formed, and by which the bent is given, in a great measure, to his Inclinations.

The Definition of Education 191

The desire of Respect or Approbation appears to be the Mainspring; and this spring, it will be found, may be made to pull in any direction.

When Captain Cook landed at Otaheite, the Education of the natives compelled them to seek the good opinion of their fellows, by the observance of several painful and ridiculous Ceremonies. The Idea, that tattooing their bodies gave them a title to general respect, was so firmly impressed on their minds, that, to gain so desirable an object, they cheerfully submitted to this painful operation;—and human nature is, and always has been, everywhere the same.

There is scarcely any inconvenience to which mankind will not submit, to gain the respect and approbation of their fellows.—And to give a right direction to this all-powerful stimulus, should be the first object of *rational Education.*

The Founder of the New System, having perceived, from the history of all nations, that this great spring was of amazing power, and *that it might be made to pull in any direction,* began to examine the bent of it in his own country, and the effects thereby produced.—He was grieved to find, that the superiority which his countrymen claimed to themselves, upon account of the correctness of their Ideas, was not admitted by other nations; and he also found, that, with them, this Great Moving Power had not been applied in the wisest manner.

The present notions of any individual cannot possibly appear absurd *to him;* but this generation can still recollect, when, among themselves, the Good Opinion of the community was obtained by the ridiculous custom of wearing a load of *false* hair, made stiff by white powder and pomatum,—when instances were known, of individuals, upon certain great occasions, spending the night in an arm-chair, with their locks frizzled in a fantastical manner, because the Hairdresser could not overtake the business that lay before him on the following day.

There is no doubt that these individuals would have lamented the taste of any one who did not admire the Wisdom of such Proceedings. They would have been offended, if they had been told that they were not acting like Rational Creatures.

These Practices were produced by the Ideas which had been impressed on their minds; and these ideas constituted their *Education*.

The present Education of this Country, or the Ideas that are generally impressed on the minds of its inhabitants, lead them all to suppose, that the Respect or Good Opinion of the Community may be obtained by the possession of money, and by what is called Rank, joined with genteel manners, and an acquaintance with the customs of polished society.—In order to be what is termed *"Respectable,"* it is necessary that the individual be not engaged in producing any thing that is either requisite or desirable. Indeed, it is even considered derogatory to his dignity, if his Forefathers, or any of his Relations, have been so employed.—Ideas of this kind constitute the present Education of what we call *Civilized Society*.

The Indians were pleased with the various figures that were tattooed on their bodies, not from any gratification that they themselves derived from these figures, but because their Friends were delighted with their appearance. Our Fathers submitted to the operations of the Hairdresser, not for the sake of the pleasure that these operations afforded, (for they were really painful,) but because *their Friends* were pleased with their appearance when so decorated. And the Young Men of our own day lace themselves up in stays, and have their dresses made

The Definition of Education

in the most fantastic manner, not for their own sakes, but through the laudable desire of giving pleasure to others. They shun every appearance of Industry or useful Employment;—or, if necessity compel them to labour, they do it in vocations that add little to the sum of human happiness; and they act thus, not from the pleasure that they derive from a mode of proceeding so manifestly absurd, but because it suits the ideas of the people; because, by this manner of acting, they obtain the good opinion of society, and it is merely owing to the prevailing system of Education, and not to its own Merits, that such a line of conduct meets with General Approbation.

Rank and money are objects of ambition upon the same ground. They are earnestly sought after, not for their intrinsic value, but because the admiration or respect of the multitude is bestowed on those who obtain them.—If it were otherwise, mankind would cease to desire them, farther than their immediate wants require.

Those who have examined this subject attentively, will have perceived, that mankind have been long upon a false scent; and that those who have been most successful in obtaining these objects, are, in point of real happiness, little better than those who want them. Like the Indians, in the operation of tattooing, the Respect or Admiration of their fellows is all they get in return for their trouble and pain. This pain and anxiety is entailed upon them by Ignorance, as the necessary consequence of a bad Education.

The *Scotsman* is correct when he says, "that the success of Mr. Owen's plan depends on his system of Education;" but he does not appear to me to have deeply studied the effects of Education, when he says, "that this is building upon straw, and binding the passions with a rope of sand."

The Education which Mr. Owen proposes to give to the children, or the ideas which he is disposed to impress upon their minds, (if I understand them correctly,) is simply, that *Knowledge and Experience,* or *virtuous and useful actions,* constitute the only just claim to Respect; and that the only Rational way to obtain the lasting Approbation of the Community, will be to aid them, and to do them good; and that the Object of *Selfishness* itself will be easiest obtained, by sinking Individual interest, and making all our Desires centre in the Good of the Community.

I shall be told, that all this is very excellent; *if it were practicable.* I answer, if we can, by Education, make people persevere in a course directly opposed to their Natural Inclinations, and hurtful to their Happiness, upon what grounds can we suppose it impracticable, by Education, to make them follow their Natural Inclination, in a course that will inevitably promote their Happiness, as long as they persevere in it?

If we can impress Ideas on their minds, that will force them to *tattoo their bodies,* to slit across their under lip, and fill the gap with a round plug of wood, or to injure their health and comfort by various Extravagancies,—if we can teach them to despise those who lodge, clothe, and feed them, and to respect those whose occupations are useless, and worse than useless,—might we not suppose it easier to form the Human Judgment upon more correct principles?

The Indians succeed in giving their notions, not only to their own children, but to the children of Europeans, when they come in their way; and these European children naturally act upon the Notions given them by the Indians.

These Notions constitute their "Education;" and unless the *Scotsman* can shew that Mr. Owen's ideas are more unnatural or absurd than the ideas of the Indians, or any other race of human beings, he will have much difficulty in proving, that a System (which makes a point of securing the Judgment and the Inclinations) is "built upon Straw."

When he takes a proper view of this subject, and begins to reflect seriously upon the source from whence he got his present Ideas, I trust that he will perceive that *the Conviction of the Judgment,* and the *formation of the Inclinations,* are the only solid foundations upon which a System can be built. And, at all events, it should be recollected, that Mr. Owen only asks for Investigation and Experiment, which can do no harm: And, when we consider the Success that attends the Indians in forming characters, we have good reason to believe that Mr. Owen will be successful also.

The children, who shall be trained under the New System, will have the Evidence of their Senses continually confirming the truth of their *Education,*—an advantage which has not been possessed by those who have gone before them.

8. William Thompson: Education in a Community

The development from Owen's ideas of a theory of Ricardian socialism was largely the work of William Thompson (1775–1833). He was an enthusiastic communitarian and wrote Practical Directions for the Speedy and Economical Establishment of Communities on the Principles of Mutual Cooperation, United Possessions and Equality, *from which this chapter, entitled "Education and Mental Pleasures," is taken.**

It would be unpardonable even during the commencement of a co-operative community, even amidst all the bustle and energy of its first exertions in the creation of the first means of comfortable existence, to pass by that great instrument, the diffusion of real knowledge to all the members, young and old, men and women, on which must depend the continuance in healthful vigour of such establishments, their salvation from the numerous enemies that would otherwise, if unprotected by knowledge, assail them.

Although during the first season, particularly if begun with such small numbers as two or three hundred per-

---

* William Thompson, *Practical Directions for the Speedy and Economical Establishment of Communities on the Principles of Mutual Cooperation, United Possessions and Equality* (London, 1830), pp. 205–225. See also p. 9, n. 14.

sons, little could be done in the way of books or regular oral instruction for adults or even for children, as well from want of leisure from indispensable active pursuits, as from want of the *materials* of instruction and of appropriate *places* in which to teach, still much may be done, even during that period, in making preparations for the diffusion of knowledge during the first winter.

The uses to which knowledge may be applied comprehend the reasons for diffusing it in the largest possible quantities, equally to all, in Co-operative Communities. These are,

1. To guard the members and their successors from the assaults of rapine or delusion, always ready under a thousand shapes from without or even from within, in the present state of things, to appropriate the fruits of their labors.

2. To enable them, not only to understand the agricultural, chemical and mechanical processes, and all the arrangements physical and social, of their establishment, with all their applications to health and comfort; but also to lead the enquiring and ingenious in particular departments amongst them, to renew and improve their machinery, processes, and arrangements, and make discoveries in all the fields of art and science, so as continually to increase their comforts, by their continually-increasing command over the animate and inanimate forces of nature as well as over their own faculties and dispositions; and to diffuse these means of increased happiness amongst their fellow-creatures.

3. To afford impartially to every member of the community the means of acquiring a new class of pleasures, *intellectual or mental pleasures,* the cheapest and easiest of acquisition, the most lasting, giving self-respect and independence to the possessors, and elevating and com-

mingling with all other pleasures physical as well as social, the only solid basis of benevolence and the only means of rendering its wishes available.

Such are briefly the reasons and purposes for which knowledge should be impartially diffused to all: the species of knowledge should be such as all mankind agree to be real and useful. Let us for our present purpose divide knowledge into two great branches, physical and moral; knowledge of things and their uses, knowledge of actions and their consequences. The first branch is again distributed into two great divisions, of—1st. things without life or minerals,—2nd. things with life or animated beings; which last are again subdivided into vegetables and animals.

FIRST BRANCH; PHYSICAL KNOWLEDGE

Knowledge of Nature, or of all existing things unchanged by human skill, called improperly Natural History.	MINERALS; including liquid and æriform fluids; their sensible properties, structure, uses, and history.
	PLANTS; their sensible properties, structure, uses, and history, called Botany.
	ANIMALS; their sensible properties, structure, uses, and history: man—his superior organization, particularly cerebral organization or that of thought; called Zoology.

ULTERIOR INVESTIGATION of the above, to acquire a still more extended and intimate knowledge of them, by

Knowledge of Nature increased	CHEMISTRY, discovering the qualities, and operations of the component parts of the preceding things on each other; producing new combinations, or simple bodies, with dissimilar qualities.

Education in a Community 199

and modified by skill in the arts of Observation and Experiment.	MECHANICS, (instead of the vague terms, natural philosophy; see Mr. Bentham's admirable work, Chrestomathia.) discovering the qualities, and operations of the preceding things, *in masses*, on each other, without change in their organization—including a knowledge of quantity and numbers (geometry and algebra) common to all bodies.

APPLICATION of the above physical knowledge to the preservation of health, to the arts, agriculture, manufactures, &c.

SECOND BRANCH; MORAL KNOWLEDGE

Distributed into two great divisions; 1st—Observations of Facts, 2nd—Rules of Conduct: thence subdivided as under.

Knowledge of Human Actions and of their Consequences; called Moral Knowlege.	OBSERVATION of human actions, and of the *consequences* of actions to the agent and all others affected by them. Moral Statistics. OBSERVATION of the processes of feelings, and of thoughts, (modifications or new species of feelings,) the antecedents and consequents of actions; called Intellectual Philosophy, or the Philosophy of the Mind. Mental Statistics. HISTORY of past *individual* actions and their consequences, called Biography, and of those of *large masses* of men called, provincial, national, universal, History. RULES for the REGULATION of the actions of *individuals*, so as to produce the greatest sum of happiness to all affected by them, unaccompanied by any other sanctions than those arising, in the existing state of society and

> knowledge, from the actions themselves; called Private Morals.
>
> RULES, LAWS, TREATIES, &c. for the REGULATION of the actions of masses of men towards each other, so as to produce the greatest sum of happiness to all affected by them, called Public Morals, and comprehending Legislation, Political Economy, Diplomacy, International Laws, &c.

APPLICATION of all the preceding physical and moral knowledge to social organization, so as to produce, by the development of all the faculties of every individual, the means of insuring permanent health for the longest life, with the means of physical, mental, and social pleasures, in the highest degree, impartially to every human being,—called SOCIAL SCIENCE.

This brief sketch, keeping clear of all disputed points, will be allowed, it is presumed, by every body, to include nothing but useful knowledge, and to be adequate to the accomplishment of the three preceding objects, to the attainment of which knowledge is the only appropriate instrument.

As we teach nothing but things, real existences, and not mere words, and as the senses are the only instruments through which such knowledge can be conveyed, we exhibit such things, animate and inanimate, to the senses of those whom we wish to instruct. Where we cannot get the things themselves, we use the best representations we can get of them, models, plans, paintings, engravings, &c. accompanying them with descriptions and demonstrations, presenting nothing to the mind that it is not capable of comprehending, proceeding from the known to the unknown, giving the materials of judgement, but always leaving the exercise of the judgement

Education in a Community

entirely free, unbiassed by hope or fear, and never demanding such long or laborious efforts of attention as to excite the repugnance of the learner.

The preceding branches of knowledge are not to be taught just in the order they are laid down, so as entirely to exclude the succeeding branches until the preceding are known. On the contrary, the rudiments of many branches of physical and moral knowledge, will be inevitably and most usefully taught together, each advancing a step as the comprehension expands. Still, much greater quantities of the preceding than of the succeeding branches will be always taught in the order stated, because they are of much easier attainment coming more immediately under the cognizance of the senses, requiring less than the succeeding of analogy or inference or abstraction, and requiring less of other branches of knowledge for their comprehension or application. In biography and history, as well as in communicating physical knowledge, there should be at least three stages of instruction in each department of knowledge; the first for children, presenting nothing but what they can comprehend and affording the data for judging accurately, without any extraneous influence of hope or fear, where judgement is required; the second for those whose minds are about half developed, midway between four or five years old and maturity; the third for those, all of whose faculties are developed or on the point of becoming so. The first biographies and histories, should contain such simple facts only as were analogous to those which the children had experienced and of the probability of which they could judge, even from their limited experience of the course of physical nature and of human actions. The second set, still relating to the same characters and events, should embrace a wider range of narrative suited to the increased knowledge of nature and social intercourse which the children would have in the meantime acquired; but biographies and histories such as they are now written, or even such as they might be written by the most intelligent and benevolent of men, and rendering the mutual massacres of men the least instead of the most interesting portions of their narratives, addressed as they naturally are to adults, occasionally embracing every department of human knowledge, and requiring a previous acquaintance with the most intricate operations of the mind, the motives to actions, and the most delicate probabilities, should not be presented to the minds of children until the close of their education; when, with no other objects but truth and a love of human happiness before them, they should be permitted to judge as calmly of past events and characters as of any existing physical circumstances or social problem around them. The same system of gradation should be followed in teaching all other branches of knowledge, physical or moral. The grand outlines, the striking subdivisions, of masses, the palpable and interesting qualities of individual bodies, should first be selected, exhibited or represented, and rendered familiar: and then, by degrees as the curiosity was excited, the pictures should be filled up and every minute part should be explored. Nothing, either physical or moral, quality, fact, and least of all opinion, should ever, at any period of its education, be presented to the mind of a child, until on the one hand, its faculties were sufficiently developed and stored with previous appropriate information, and until on the other sufficient data were afforded it of forming an accurate view or judgement; and even then the impression, conclusion, or inference, should be left entirely free, and no factitious motive should be permitted to distract or bias

Education in a Community 203

its attention, or in any way influence its conclusions. If our objects in education be the happiness of the child and the investigation of the truth as an essential instrument for attaining that happiness, this will be our method. If we have other objects, different means will be employed. Wherever the means of judging are not afforded, *no opinion* should be formed. Wherever the means of judging are not afforded, the formation of opinions is generally pernicious, always immaterial. If the formation of opinions on any subject be important, thence arises the importance of affording the means of forming an unbiassed judgment, not of forming opinions without reason.

But—how shall we induce the children to acquire all this useful knowledge, casting aside as we do the influence of physical or mental pain, force or terror, from our motives to exertion? First—as to the matters to be taught, we reject every thing uninteresting to children; next, as to the mode of teaching, we reject all painful feelings and associations and use exclusively those that are pleasing.

Thus, *as we teach nothing but what is agreeable,* we never burden the memory with names of things not known, or phrases not understood, but either occupy the senses with observing the properties of things or afford the pleasures of mental activity exercised on the properties so discovered and suited to the state of development of the mind. We substitute the teaching of things and demonstration for the teaching of words and mere memory. We teach *all* the qualities of bodies, instead of merely *two,* namely those of quantity and numbers (which are in truth but the *one, of quantity,* increased or diminished, the most abstract and the most difficult, as now taught, to be understood,) now, sometimes, taught in schools, and the only useful things taught there, under the exclusive and vaunted name of *science:* and we repress by all useful means, (instead of encouraging by all species of factitious rewards and punishments) the imbecility of mind which affects to be convinced without understanding, never biassing the judgment of the pupils on *any* subject, nor forcing our own conclusions upon them. Where a child cannot yet judge of a proposition, we say nothing about it, we do not ask it to form any *opinion* until it shall have acquired the materials of judging, and we direct its attention in the meantime to those simple matters on which it is prepared to institute comparisons and to judge. We know that the mind of a child can no more resist the formation of just conclusions when the materials of judging are afforded it and when no factitious motives or associations are used to influence its judgment, than it can the formation of any conclusions the teacher wishes when the means of judging are withheld from it and when factitious motives (any motives but those arising out of the evidence itself) are used to influence its decisions.

Next, *as to the mode of teaching*. We gratify the love of motion and activity of body and mind of all children from infancy upwards, their love of novelty and curiosity, by surrounding their places of instruction by pleasant gardens for their use, by requiring the attention but for a short period at a time increasing with their desire to learn, by the exhibition and examination of things themselves, their models, or pictured representations, by teaching the hands of all to sketch or draw the objects presented to them, by giving them practical illustrative and demonstrative operations to perform, by varying their school amusements with those of industry, with useful operations suited to their years, in the gardens, fiields, or manufactories, where their parents and friends

Education in a Community 205

are always ready to receive and direct them; as well as by the additional variety of music, dancing, and all other healthful gymnastic exercises, not with the view of developing mere strength, but of obtaining an easy command of all the muscular faculties for useful purposes, by teaching the more advanced of them to prepare amongst their relations and friends, the machine-makers of the Community, to renew, improve upon, and always keep up with their own hands, the instruments, drawings, models, &c. necessary to elucidate and render intelligible the information addressed to them, by shewing them, in the industrious pursuits of the community and their own, the application and practice of the facts and principles established in the course of their instruction, by soliciting from them questions and enquiry by colloquial instruction, by teaching the children to instruct each other, by shewing them at every step the *uses* of knowledge, and to crown all, by unruffled serenity, kindness, and firmness, and by an undeviating example of the practice of every thing we recommend.

Such being the things to be taught, and such the mode of teaching, what are the motives that are to lead the children to find pleasure in learning such matters? Adequate motives will perhaps present themselves on the mere previous statement, to most persons. The most important then, of the tutelary or useful principles of influence or motives to exertion or learning, are the following. They are simply the desire to experience again (after having once experienced them) the following pleasures; viz.,

The pleasures of *activity or exertion*.

The pleasures of *sympathy*.

The prospective pleasures of *utility,* in anticipation of the consequential *uses* to which knowledge may be applied: frequently the actual pleasures of experienced utility.

These constitute perhaps or comprehend all the motives than can be employed usefully, or without preponderant evil, in education, and are quite abundant and of sufficient energy for all useful purposes, without resorting to those of a doubtful, much less those of a demonstrated pernicious, tendency.

The *pernicious* motives, are factitious rewards and punishments, particularly the latter, physical pain and terror: to these has been added of late years, the principle of *Emulation;* which, where physical pain and terror have been abolished, is generally substituted for them. We regard emulation as a principle of education, not much superior to factitious rewards and punishments, founding, as it does, the gratification of one individual on the relative inferiority of others. The *moral* evil of the principle, utterly hostile as it is to benevolence, which would rejoice in every species of good to another —the only condition on which that other can rejoice in every species of good to ourselves—entirely overbalances, in our opinion, any intellectual benefits which emulation is supposed to produce: which benefits, however, may be obtained much more effectually, and to an incalculably greater number of pupils, by other useful means.

The principle, whose tendency is doubtful, and which we would therefore exclude as superfluous, is the very powerful principle, powerful to evil as are all the above pernicious principles, the principle of arbitrary *Association*. Where are the ferocious antipathies, where are the prejudices of party and colour, where are the imbecility and prostration of mind, that do not owe their chief origin to the fatal use in the hands of ignorance and passion, of the tremendous power of early association? throwing over objects no way connected, the good or the evil of any other objects real or imaginary, as the wildest or weakest caprice may dictate, binding up for ever in its adamantine knot the powers of future discrimination, and frequently rendering the life of its victim, as well as of those amongst whom it is thrown, wretched? Objects should be presented to the mind, as they exist, *in their own forms and colours*. Association always presents them with the glow of other colours not belonging to them. We object to association therefore that its premeditated and factitious exercise, joining things together which are not united in nature as cause and effect or in any other manner, necessarily implies a *falsehood;* and also that it is an instrument peculiarly liable to the misuse of the wicked and foolish, while the wise and benevolent have no need of it.

The rose pleases from its colours, its form, and its fragrance. It asks no aid from association to render it lovely and beloved. We wish however to make the couch-grass or the dock-leaf equally agreeable to a child. We therefore present the two to it always together; and either by the continued assertion of some falsehood respecting some imputed virtue of the weed, as of its power to cure disease or to influence future events, or the practical falsehood of always connecting together the stems of the flower and the weed, neatly joined together, and feeling ourselves (if under the influence of the same early association) or, if not, affecting to feel, an equal delight in the flower and the weed, we imbue the child's mind with an associated love of what is pernicious.

Is not this mode of teaching, whether applied to things or to human actions, a gross injustice towards those on whom it is practised? Why should not the qualities of individual things, be judged apart from all other things, nicely discriminated and weighed? How else can we acquire truth or a knowledge of the *real* relations and qualities of things? What but mischief to the judgment, can be produced by this association, this jumbling of qualities?

It is wished to teach children geometry, some notions of mental philosophy or other more abstruse matters, for forming an accurate judgment of which their minds are not yet prepared. Instead of waiting until their minds are more developed and then presenting calmly to them the materials for judging, we put the matters we wish them to learn (that is to get by heart) into rhythm, make them repeat it with regular cadence, introduce pleasingly soft or agitating music, and confound in the children's minds the pleasures of the accompaniments with an associated affection for the notions so inculcated. What folly or wickedness could we not make agreeable by such meretricious means? If *we* make use of music and decoration and the colours and luxury of dress, to aid in inculcating *our* notions and rendering them more impressive, how can we object to those who use the same means to intoxicate men with a delight in, what they call the glory of, the wholesale slaughter of their fellow-creatures?

We most carefully distinguish, however, arbitrary Association, from *combined pleasures,* or the union of pleasing things, or of things pleasing and unpleasing. By combining pleasing things, the individual qualities of each being previously scrutinized and known, each may be made to give a mutual charm to the other, and the disagreeable impressions from unpleasant objects, known to be such, may be relieved (when they cannot be removed) by the vicinity of those that are pleasing.

Education in a Community

What distinguishes arbitrary association and constitutes its vice in education, is, that the impressions from one object are substituted, and by the mind mistaken, for those from another. So understood—which seems to be its proper meaning in this place—Association, like Emulation, is universally pernicious in education.

There remain therefore, as purely useful motives to the acquisition of knowledge, for adults as well as for the young, the desire of the pleasures of Activity, or the Exercise of the faculties, muscular or mental, of Sympathy, and of Utility, of the anticipated, or consequential, as well as of the immediate, Uses of knowledge. What minor pleasures do these heads include?

1. PLEASURES of ACTIVITY, or the exercise of the faculties, includes, first of all, all the *pleasures of the senses* that are called into use by such activity, those of the eye, the touch, the ear, the taste, &c.; next, the *pleasures of muscular exertion* grateful and conducive to the health of adults but a delight quite indispensable to the young; and last, the *pleasures of the exercise of the mental powers*, which with many adults, almost supersede all other pleasures and which even in children, were they permitted to compare and judge freely of all things, and not forced into premature judgment of any thing, would become an ever increasing source of delight.

Pleasures of Novelty. Next to the above pleasures which may be indefinitely repeated, follow a class included also under the head of Activity, now almost peculiar to the young, called, the pleasures of novelty. An agreeable impression made for the first time, is an ascertained possible addition to our stock of future pleasures. The impression, not only from its difference in kind, but from our consciousness of its not having been felt before, operates more vividly, and generally more pleasantly on the mind. Every new fact, every new quality of things, every new mode of action and ascertained consequences, until the prodigality of the objects of art and nature and their qualities are exhausted, is thus a natural reward, in the hand of the skilful and benevolent teacher, to gratify his pupils.

Pleasures of Curiosity. Having once and again experienced the pleasures of novelty, the pupil wishes for more and more of such pleasures. Instead of repressing this inclination, we shall make it as useful as delightful; and *nothing* in the whole domain of things that a child feels an interest in enquiring about, shall be withheld from its scrutinizing glance, well assured that a child if left to itself, will soon cease to push its enquiries where it cannot comprehend.

Pleasures of Discovery. But some children are not satisfied with mere curiosity, with wishing for novelties and waiting until they come to them. They set out in quest of new pleasures, sometimes without any particular species in chase, sometimes as intent on some particular species as was Columbus in daring the unmeasured expanse of the Atlantic, and equally, though not so durably or philosophically, delighted with the success of the adventure. This species of pleasure, where the circumstances surrounding children are not only compatible with, but inviting to, its exercise, may also be so directed by the teacher acquainted with the rudiments of the knowledge of all *things* and anxious to communicate what he knows, as to increase, at the same time, the knowledge and the happiness of the pupils. Such pleasures would be substituted for the drudgery of unintelligible grammars and *dead* languages, which young children cannot be made to learn but by compulsion; but which may, at a more advanced age, be learned, if necessary, by an improved method, in a few months; and whose only use and effect as now prematurely, exclusively, and unskilfully taught, seems to be to disgust children with all, even real and useful, knowledge. The greater part of the qualities and uses of bodies, the matters to be taught children, may thus be discovered by the children themselves, their attention being once excited and directed to the pursuit, and the means of making the discovery judiciously facilitated to them.

Pleasures of Invention, of Planning. As education advances from a knowledge of the qualities of things, to an acquaintance with the chemical and mechanical contrivances by which those qualities have been rendered of such increased utility beyond what their first sensible appearances promised, the pupils, if well directed, will all, more or less, wish to experience the active mental and muscular pleasures of inventing and planning, themselves; and in the fields, in the workshops, and amongst the machines and the adult friends around them, they would find all the materials for the development of their inventive powers. Many a false calculation, many a contrivance that would excite a smile, but a smile of pleasure and of encouragement to persevere, would be exhibited; but the pleasures of activity, the habit of useful exertion, the development of the faculties would proceed, and thus would the object of education be gained, though the plans and inventions failed. This inclination also the teacher would in every way encourage and aid with kindly suggestions to regulate its efforts to the most useful purposes; showing the children what had been done in the same line, and how the effects of their errors had been obviated.

2. PLEASURES OF SYMPATHY. This is another of the great principles, or motives to improvement, that may

be safely used in education, or in communicating knowledge to adults. To prevent abuse, however,—for even Sympathy as well as arbitrary Association, though not to the same extent, is liable to abuse—it must be always used in conjunction with and secondary to our two other modes of influence, namely the pleasures of Activity, just noticed, and those of Reason or the prospective pleasures of Utility, to be presently mentioned: Reason or judgment should be exercised by the child as soon as, and in proportion as, its powers are developed, and in the mean time by the tutor looking forward solely to the happiness of the child, for its preservation, not to control its judgment.

Sympathy is not a mere branch of Association: it is on the contrary on the inevitable feelings of sympathy that the wonder-working powers of Association are founded. Sympathy is a secondary feeling of pleasure or of pain necessarily arising in the minds of infants on perceiving the union of the feeling, or of the expression of the feeling, of pleasure or pain by another, with the feeling of pleasure or pain immediately by themselves. These two sets of feelings of different individuals having been frequently experienced at the same time, (as in the act of giving milk by the mother to the infant, the mother feeling pleasure from the relief the withdrawing of the milk affords, the infant from the gratification of taste and appetite afforded by the milk,) it so happens that when either of the previously united feelings or expressions of feeling, as the smile of the mother, occurs separately, a part of the previous united pleasure is, by the human nervous organization, excited with it. This feeling of pleasure excites in its turn a disposition to please, to give pleasure in return to, the person exciting it. Hence the instantaneous and involuntary pleasure in

Education in a Community 213

the minds of all persons whom perverse circumstances have not *un*educated, in witnessing the expression or reality of happiness, and of pain in witnessing the expression or the reality of pain, in others. Hence the origin of sympathy: it is a feeling necessarily acquired by all, with hardly an exception, in the course of the education of circumstances. The exercise of sympathy is confined to *persons:* association may extend its capricious bonds of union over all things in nature, or even out of nature, as well as over persons. The feeling of sympathy is unavoidable, and ordinarily as useful as pleasing: but if not guided by reason, even it may degenerate into a mere animal impulse, a species of instinct, regardless of the future and blind to consequences.

Sympathy is the basis on which benevolence and beneficence (or benevolence carried into action) have been usually built. Even without any previous sympathy however—of which, nevertheless, it would be almost as difficult as destructive to our happiness to endeavour to divest ourselves—we may be beneficent to an unlimited extent, from mere observation of the effects or consequences of beneficent actions, not only affording immediate pleasure in their exercise, but from their tendency to attract the kindly feelings and actions of all around (when not thwarted by a fortuitous host of *artificial* adverse circumstances) towards the individual happiness of those who practice them. Sympathy, the necessary offspring of mutual interest leading to mutuality of pleasure, and parent in its turn of mutual kindness without end, should be nurtured and encouraged in the minds of children: but no efforts should be made unduly to exalt the feeling towards any particular individual, nor beyond the demand of the peculiar circumstances of the case. If this feeling be too highly excited, it will mar the exercise of the judgment on all subjects with which it has had any sort of connexion, not to speak of the general effect of all excessive stimuli in producing debilitating, if not painful reaction. Therefore as the understanding becomes developed, the direction of sympathy should be regulated by a review of the remote as well as the immediate consequences of actions, exhibiting frequently a future pain tremendously overbalancing a present pleasure, even of sympathy. If the feelings of sympathy be so blindly cultivated as to incapacitate children from judging of the good or the bad qualities of those persons towards whom they are directed, they degenerate into *false associations* respecting persons, clothing with all good qualities those who have pleased the children, and with all evil qualities those who have, justly or unjustly, displeased them. The moral as well as intellectual evils liable to arise from this source, are beyond calculation. The beloved tutor of superior knowledge, in whose favor sympathy is unduly excited, holds prostrate the understanding of his pupils, and turns their affections, their love and their hatred, to whatever persons or objects he wills.

Sympathy, it is true, has its pains as well as its pleasures; but its pains are always relieved by wishing to relieve the unhappiness that caused them, by studying the means of relieving it, and when opportunity and ability offer, by practising those means. When the causes of painful sympathy are irremediable, its pains, like our immediate sufferings, are as tranquilly as possible, borne, till the mind can be diverted to other objects. If a teacher or those around children, give them the example of expressing no feelings but those of regret and compassion at unpleasing qualities in others, it will never form antipathies, will never harbour ill-will, malice, or re-

Education in a Community

venge: it will enjoy all the pleasures and the uses of sympathy without any of the pains and mischiefs of antipathy.

Neither sympathy nor any other of our feelings, (whether originally existing in the capabilities of our organization, or necessarily called into exercise by external circumstances through which all must pass, or the joint effect of circumstances acting on universal or peculiar organization,) should ever be so far cultivated as to incapacitate children, as their powers of discriminating and judging advance, from calmly enquiring into the circumstances which originally gave rise to them, and into the *consequences* of their indulgence on every particular occasion. Sympathy unduly excited in children towards any particular individual, though altogether benevolent towards that individual, may be the parent of cruelty, not the less intense because unpremeditated, towards every other person.

Sympathy, therefore, as an instrument of education, may be abused, though not to the extent to which association may be abused, except when it is made the basis on which false associations are founded. Against this abuse, if possible to any extent, we must guard. The simple mode is, to make sympathy always, as much as possible, go hand in hand with a perception of the good qualities which excite and justify it, to regulate, restrain, or increase, its energy on every occasion by a prospective view of its consequences, and to encourage by all wise means and on every occasion, universal sympathy and kindness towards all companions, instead of isolated groups of individual capricious attachments.

Opposed to Sympathy stands the antagonist principle of *Antipathy*. Sympathy is the feeling of pleasure or of pain which we experience when we perceive, or hear of, other people experiencing pleasure or pain: it is always attended with benevolence towards the persons exciting it.

As sympathy leads us to feel pleasure at the happiness of others and to feel pain at their distresses; so, on the contrary, would antipathy train us to feel pleasure at the distresses of others and pain at their happiness. Antipathy is a feeling of dislike to certain persons, without any just ground even of disapprobation in the mind of the person feeling the antipathy: the range of antipathy is limited to the painful affections: what are called its pleasures, are nothing else but the keen desire of getting rid, and almost always in a manner confirming and embittering them, of the tormenting feeling with which it goads us: it is always attended with malevolence towards the persons ever so innocently exciting it. Sympathy may therefore be cultivated without the cultivation at the same time of the principle of Antipathy. Antipathy is one of the most pernicious branches of the fruitful tree (fruitful in moral as well as intellectual evil) of false or erroneous Association. If we dismiss from our motives, or springs of action, the main trunk of arbitrary Association, we shall, as included in it and as one of the worst of its dependents, dismiss the principle of Antipathy, in education as well as in the whole of life. Antipathy is now used to a fearful extent in education as well as through the whole intercourse of life, leading one half of mankind to feel aversion to the other half, because they differ in wealth, in length of time during which wealth or power have been possessed by their respective predecessors, because they differ from them in place of birth, in belief, in colour, in artificial or conventional manners; without any regard to those moral and intellectual qualities, which should form the sole estimate of judging individual worth; but, which

Education in a Community

even wanting, should excite no other feelings than those of compassion, regret, and anxious desire, impelling to action, to implant every where those useful qualities which, in proportion to their diffusion, must render all happy. As we not only remove from children all the circumstances which generate antipathies, but direct all their feelings towards persons into the opposite channels of sympathy, and never ourselves disapprove before them without a reason, we fear no more the springing up of antipathies towards persons than the likings or dislikings of inanimate things without the perception of any pleasing or unpleasing qualities in them.

Sympathy has, as we have said, its pains as well as pleasures. Antipathy has no real pleasures: its temporary gratifications are mingled with bitterness in their apparent enjoyment, and are followed by consequences multiplying evils without end. Even the pains of sympathy, few as they may be under well-arranged circumstances, and when restrained by utility, are ever relieved by the prospective aspect of the mitigation or utter banishment of the evils which excite them, and by the active exertion of the faculties which such prospective aspect calls forth.

So guarded, sympathy, the physical basis, if we may so call it, of beneficence, becomes a moral principle of action, and as such we use it as one of our motives to exertion. It is evident however that the whole intellectual benefit expected from the use of such an instrument as sympathy, must depend on the direction given to it, and this again on the *example* of those in whose favor sympathy has been excited. From sympathy and from example then (or the frequent exercise in a particular way of the physical or intellectual faculties before those whom it is wished to influence) spring,

The pleasures of imitation. The tendency to imitation, so universal in children, is not simply an effect of the love of the pleasures of sympathy but of the pleasures of activity combined with those of sympathy. So strong is this principle, even in adults, that very few persons thrown into a new society, though much differing from their previous habits, can resist the good or the bad influence of example, can refuse to imitate what every one around them practices. Great energy of mind, invincible habit, or strong cultivation of reason, are necessary in adults to resist the whirlpool of example. What then can children—whose habits are to be formed, whose reason is to be cultivated, whose plastic natures only pant for action, almost indifferent to the direction or future consequences of activity provided its immediate mode of development be pleasurable—what can children do to oppose the all surrounding currents of example?; how can they refuse to imitate what they see done by all around them, whether gentle or ferocious, whether reasonable or absurd? Activity of some sort is indispensable to their physical temperament. A mode of exercising that activity is displayed before them, the difficulty of finding out this mode is removed, the pleasures of activity are afforded, and they are rewarded for joining in the common pursuits not only by the pleasures of activity but by the approving sympathy of their companions and the superior and controlling sympathy of their tutors. When all these modes of influence are conjoined, their operation over the minds and conduct of children are irresistable. The teacher however, besides his sympathy with the useful and pleasurable development of the children's active faculties, should himself be interested, should feel a pleasure, in what he teaches and in the progress of teaching, or he will lose half the effect of the power of sympathy.

Education in a Community

Thus selecting for teaching those matters only which are fitted to the actual state of development of the physical and mental powers of children, which are therefore always agreeable to them, and which will prove the most useful to them, their happiness on its comprehensive scale being our sole and sincere object, excluding all the immediately painful as well as the consequentially injurious modes of influence, and using those only which bear the touchstone of permanent utility as well as of immediate gratification, we shall find in our hands such sources of gentle but irresistable power over the susceptible minds and habits of children as to make us fearful of the misuse, even with the best intentions, of such power by ourselves. *We,* of the co-operative school, believe, on the evidence of our senses and experience that the compound resulting from the peculiarities of organization of the mass of children (comparatively limited,) is *necessarily* modified by the compound (almost unlimited) resulting from the peculiarities of the circumstances surrounding and acting on that organization; and that therefore the circumstances being supposed in our power, and sufficient skill being supposed in us to wield them aright, it is *possible* for us to form children into any characters, wise or foolish, kindly or malicious. The pleasures of sympathy may be abused: even the pleasures of activity may be misdirected into any one species, as that of mere muscular excitement. Amongst those who think that within children is placed a mysterious power of counteracting the influence of organization and of external circumstances, there may be some consistency in seizing all weapons that present themselves to crush such a monster of human nature as this unmotivated self-directing power, in so weak a receptacle. But for us, who know the power we possess over the plastic minds of children, and who sincerely wish to teach them nothing but truth, or the real properties and relations of things and the consequences of actions, that they may, by the proper use of them, attain to happiness,—shall we not tremble lest we misuse such powers of influence, shall we not anxiously look out for the best remedy that the nature of things affords, to be placed if possible in the hands of children themselves, as a check on such abuse?

Acknowledging and maintaining as we do the all-commanding influence of circumstances in the formation of character, according to the modifications of each particular organization, we therefore, acknowledge also and maintain the necessity of *checks* on the misuse of so tremendous a power; checks to be placed as it were in the hands of the taught themselves. Those who suppose that, within children themselves resides some mysterious internal power of resisting the effect of external circumstances on their feelings, opinions, and actions, and of self-forming their character in spite of external agencies, such persons may indeed be justified as consistent at least in making use of all factitious means of influence to subdue to their views this capricious unreasoning principle. But for us, who maintain the necessary and appropriate influence of circumstances, well or ill arranged, in promoting vice or virtue, truth or error, and who maintain that *truth* or an accurate perception of things as they really exist as well as of the consequences resulting from their living actions of inanimate properties (whether our opinions coincide with such perceptions, or not,) is essential to human happiness, not to interpose checks on the mere influence of *opinions* through sympathy, awe, or any species of association, would be fatally inconsistent indeed.

Education in a Community 221

Therefore, as one, and perhaps the most important, of the bases of moral as of intellectual education, *to every child should be guaranteed the free development of its powers, and the free exercise of its judgment on every thing laid before it, without inspiring it with any sentiment either of hatred or respect for any existing opinion or belief.* In Miss Frances Wright's amiable and spirited exposition of the principles of her co-operative establishment at Nashoba, Tennessee, on the east bank of the Mississippi, in conjunction with General La Fayette and some other enlightened individuals, for educating and improving the blacks equally with the whites, this guarantee of mental liberty is given.

3. PROSPECTIVE PLEASURES *of the consequential* USES, *to which knowledge may be applied;* or pleasures of UTILITY. In the cultivation of this source of pleasure as the minds of children become developed, coupled with the above cautious mode of using the pleasures of sympathy and even those of activity, we shall find the best guard to children against the misdirection of their faculties, against the formation of erroneous judgments, or of any opinions without appropriate evidence. In truth, though the pleasures of utility as motives to improvement, may be separately discussed and last in order, and though the chief efficiency of each set of motives, may be in the order stated; yet from the earliest period of education must they be all used, sometimes together, more frequently in succession, to promote the ultimate general effect. A regard to ultimate utility to any great extent, must evidently be the result of very considerable development of the faculties: but, when acquired, it becomes so powerful a motive to exertion as altogether to supersede dependence on the immediate pleasures of activity or of sympathy. This regard to ultimate use,

therefore, should, on every occasion, be called forth, not only as an additional motive to exertion, but as a corrective to the undue force of the preceding motives, as well as to their misdirection. Where the teaching of things not useful for the ordinary purposes of life, as of mere languages and literature or metaphysical dogmas, is made the basis of education; or where even nothing but useful matters, and with appropriate materials for teaching, are taught, but where such knowledge is *not necessary* to the pupils to enable them to acquire and enjoy what should be the fruit of their own appropriate exertions; (as where useful things are taught to those children, all of whose wants are and will be supplied to excess without any need of exertion of mind or muscle on their part) in either of these cases, the motives to improvement arising from the prospective pleasures of the uses to which knowledge may be applied, must be either altogether annihilated or reduced to a mere weak curiosity requiring long-continued training and application for its gratification. It is only under such an arrangement of social circumstances as shall permit nothing but what is useful to be taught, as shall use none but cheerful motives to exertion, as shall be possessed of the varied and extensive materials and machinery, mental and physical, necessary to convey this useful knowledge, and above all as shall render necessary to the future happiness of life the acquisition of such knowledge, and shall render such happiness a necessary consequence of such acquisition, that the motives to improvement, or to the acquisition of knowledge, arising from the utility of such improvement, can produce their full effect. But where all these circumstances are combined, and where the uses of knowledge in every department can be so plainly and immediately demonstrated by reference to the industrial

Education in a Community

operations on every side surrounding the pupils, as can be done in co-operative communities, how can we now well conceive the extent and operation to which such motives to improvement, under such circumstances, may be carried? If children are not only permitted but encouraged to demand the uses of every thing, if their judgments are on all occasions left entirely free, the tutor doing no more than affording the best materials at his command for forming right judgments, if our sincere object be to teach the truth and nothing but truth, and least of all to teach our opinions, or any opinions, without appropriate evidence, and that evidence be left to work its own way, we shall have done every thing in our power to guard the children from the errors likely to arise from undue reliance on our intellectual superiority or from an over-excited desire of commanding our sympathy: and the errors into which they may still fall, will rather arise from the defective state of human knowledge and of the means of communicating it, than from any usurpation of teachers over the mental liberty of children.

Keeping steadily in view the things to be taught, the modes and the materials of teaching and the modes made use of to induce to learn, as attempted to be explained above, we shall perceive at once the best use to which the first season could be applied by those members of the community, say five, whose chief occupation should be to instruct. All of these should be employed during the first season, in preparing the materials for future instruction, such as chemical and philosophical apparatus, in collecting minerals, plants and animals, or forming preparations of animals and plants, in drawing up lessons or courses of moral, intellectual, and social instruction, with physical illustrations. Some of these teachers might be at the same time practical chemists, physicians, or surgeons, accountants, engineers, &c. and might thus in a double capacity be useful. It would be very desirable that they should be able to make with their own hands many of the chemical and mechanical implements and apparatus. One person skilled, or at least able to make himself skilled, in natural history, another in mechanics, and another in chemistry, or at least one person having a general knowledge of all the three, would be quite indispensable, along with one person chiefly employed in the moral sciences, particularly the general principles of education, or the formation of moral and intellectual character. All these should constantly communicate together, that their modes of teaching both young and old, might, in their several departments, harmonize together, rendering each other mutual aid and information; no circumstances existing around them to cause any rivalry or opposition of interests. It would be most desirable that all of the teachers should be able to draw, if not to paint, that they might prepare drawings of what they could not exhibit in nature or by models, as drawings of plants, animals, machines frequently on the scale of life or reality, particularly explaining those in use, in the different lines of manufacturing industry, natural phenomena, striking events in history or biography, processes of art in draining, mining, gardening &c. &c. If the teachers could not themselves sketch, young persons instructed in the useful art of drawing, should be particularly invited to join the community, and should aid the teachers in their art, receiving from them their particular knowledge, and thus preparing themselves for giving future instruction along with the teachers. It would perhaps be better, at the beginning, even to do without teachers than without

Education in a Community 225

draftsmen and modellers. Drawing should be also one of the permanent, most pleasing and therefore most useful, of the modes and aids to instruction in all departments. The *materials* for drawing, modelling, implement and instrument-making, would be all that the community would have to contribute towards the preparation for future instruction: the rest would be the product of that species of labor which is necessary to prepare for communicating knowledge in the different departments.

It must not be supposed however that because little or no formal instruction can be given during the first six or eight busy months of a Co-operative Community beginning with funds so limited as £20 a head, that therefore no real or useful knowledge can be communicated to the members. On the contrary, they will be every day acquiring useful *practical* knowledge, learning from and teaching each other. Theirs will be eminently the *education of circumstances*. Unlike the arrangements of competitive industry in general society, every one will be interested to teach every one what he knows. Whoever is skilled in the science or in the art of agriculture, of gardening, of building, of woollen cloth, of silk, of hardware, of machine-making, will be anxious to make all around as intelligent and as skilful as him or herself, because by such communication of knowledge and skill, over and above the direct pleasure of such social and intellectual intercourse, the labors of the intelligent and skilful will by such communication be abridged, and their enjoyments in the same proportion increased by the increased production consequent on the universal diffusion of knowledge and skill in every department of industry. It will not only be the interest of these occupied in the same trades, in the same employments, to aid and instruct each other, but it will be equally the interest of those employed within doors to communicate their knowledge and skill to those ordinarily employed, (particularly until the community is completed and independent) without, not fearing that their trade will be overstocked and that those whom they teach may hereafter supplant them in competition for the means of existence. In return, these employed without, will be anxious for the efficient aid whenever necessary of those ordinarily within doors, and will be anxious to render that aid as useful as possible for their own and the universal benefit. Daily occasional intercourse, also, of all with those who understand the whole of the co-operative arrangements and their connexion with each other, and with those who understand all the machines in use, the rationale of the agricultural, chemical, and domestic processes, will aid in diffusing useful knowledge in the most engaging way to all the members. The motives to learn and to acquire skill will be also altogether different from those which now exist. It is now a matter of mere idle curiosity, for which gratification even, never ending toil affords no respite, in one tradesman to inquire into the operations of another, or even into the principles of the operations which his own hands perform. Of whom shall he learn skill, even in his own art, when every one round him is his competitor?

Equally efficient as in communicating practical physical knowledge and in exciting a desire for the future regular and systematic development of it, will co-operative arrangements be, in giving birth to mutual good will and to every moral habit. When interest, real or supposed, is not promoted by mutual annoyance, mutual annoyance will cease to be practised: where interest, immediate and palpable, requires mutual aid, and where

Education in a Community 227

such interest is promoted to the greatest extent, by the utmost perfection of knowledge, of skill, and of conduct, in all around, there will be mutual aid, and mutual instruction and benevolence will flourish. Where every want is gratified by light and pleasing exertion, & where there are no means of gratifying the capricious and short-sighted desires of intemperance and other vices but by additional labor directed to the procuring of the means of their gratification, this natural price and penalty will be deemed too dear a purchase, and even the short-sighted will quickly lose the desire of such enjoyments on such terms, attended as they would be by the repulsive absence of the sympathy of their companions, in their pernicious gratification and display.

Besides the various knowledge thus incidentally conveyed during the first fine-weather working season, by the mere operation of the arrangements of a co-operative community, constituting a great *practical school,* ever efficient in enlarging the mind and harmonizing the disposition, working unseen, without the formal announcement of any specific purpose, without the display of any artificial punishments or rewards, every effect following from the silent influence of judiciously combined physical and moral causes, exciting no personal jealousies, nor humiliations; advantage will be taken, the very first winter, of the many spare unemployed hours of the season when all are congregated within doors to teach every individual of the community not acquainted with those arts, to read, to write, and the elements of figures, that they may be able, by means of books, to acquire knowledge for themselves, as well as to communicate that knowledge or passing events to others. By means of the facilities afforded by the judicious methods of Pestalozzi, Hamilton, and others, reading, writing or spelling the words in ordinary use, may be conveyed in a few dozen lessons. Thus may all the members be raised one important step in the intellectual scale, respecting themselves, and taking away the temptation from those, to whom competition and accidents had previously given the means of acquiring such mental arts, of regarding them with the too-readily re-excited antipathies of superiority. During the winter also, all may attend lectures explaining the general principles of social organization, the co-operative as contrasted with the competitive system of industry, the actual state of the community as compared with their prospective and ultimate state of independence, improvement, and happiness, the habits necessary to be formed by all the members to produce in the shortest time the happiest results. Besides these and many other social topics to be addressed to the members by those capable of conveying them, and to be afterwards discussed in the way of question and examination of those so inclined, the teachers of physical science may begin, if not regular courses in their several departments, at least so much of the explanation and application to use of minerals, vegetables, and animals, of their general knowledge of chemistry, and mechanics, as may be necessary to enable all to understand, and thus to increase their interest in, the several occupations of agriculture, gardening, building, manufactures, domestic economy, in which they have been engaged, looking forward also to those in which they are to be engaged the succeeding year; along with the general rules and the reasons of them, for the preservation of health, and an outline of the functions of the human organization; thus exciting the curiosity for a more extensive acquaintance, on a systematic plan, under the name of science,

Education in a Community

at a future period when more ample means shall have been provided for general education. The more simple these first courses of instruction, the more level to the comprehension of children of twelve years old to adult age, the better. Those whose knowledge extends beyond them, can improve themselves, and can aid by conversation or any other method to improve others. To those adults who have never had the means of acquiring such knowledge, the difficulties of learning will be quite as great, and in some cases greater, than those of young persons: the necessity of simplifying knowledge therefore to the utmost possible extent, will be equally great for both classes of learners, the young and the adult. One of the corridors, above or below stairs, will perhaps serve as the most convenient place of teaching until an appropriate place is provided, the illustrative drawings, sections, sectional as well as entire models, &c. being placed across the passage in the way of a scene, and the whole space warmed for the time with a stove. These instructions at the same time will not interfere with the regular progress of industry.

A circumstance which gives the greatest facility to the diffusion of knowledge in a co-operative community, is the needlessness of very profound knowledge, in the commencement, in the teachers themselves. Very profound or learned teachers, particularly if their knowledge be confined to any one department, are apt in giving lectures or lessons, to aim more at the display, to the gratification of an idle personal vanity, of their own learning and profundity, than at the communication of their knowledge in the most simple, and therefore efficient and expeditious, manner, to those who hear them. The small demands, in the beginning, on those who teach in a community, (where almost all, though the most intelligent and best disposed of the existing industrious classes, necessarily set out in the state of almost utter ignorance in which they have been brought up in general society) will give such teachers the opportunity of studying and improving themselves as they proceed, of enlarging and improving their own minds as they improve those of others. Thus good teachers will be found fully as fast as the increased desire and capability of receiving knowledge on the part of the taught, can require their services. Thus easily, with the aid of the best publications, may be supplied the demand for instruction of such communities.

9. William Maclure: Opinions on Various Subjects

So substantial were Maclure's contributions to the experiment at New Harmony that he may almost be considered a cofounder of the community with Owen. He made a large financial investment in the village, and he persuaded several distinguished scientists to make New Harmony their headquarters. It was Maclure's library, equipment, and collections of natural history that provided the necessary basis for scientific teaching and research. The practical success of the schools at New Harmony was the work of a small band of Pestalozzian teachers whom Maclure supported; and the School of Industry was the result of his special concern to provide "useful" as opposed to "ornamental" education. The observations reprinted below were written in 1826–1828.

Education may be divided into two species, like mankind; that is, the productive and non-productive, the useful and ornamental, the necessary and amusing, &c. &c. It is the productive, useful and necessary, that constitutes the comfort and happiness of the millions, and ought alone to occupy the care and attention of all representative governments, elected by the majority of the

---

* William Maclure, *Opinions on Various Subjects* (3 vols.; New Harmony, Ind., 1831–1838), I, 48–67. See also p. 10, n. 17.

millions, who produce all that is consumed under the denomination either of public or private revenue. The millions have a right to what they produce; and all appropriations out of the public treasury, for teaching the non-productive knowledge which is merely ornamental or amusing to the possessor, may perhaps be considered as a deviation from right and justice, in expending the fruit of the labour and toil of the productive classes, to teach the children of the idle and non-productive, how to consume their own time and the public property, in learning to amuse themselves and kill time agreeably.

As the greatest part of what is taught in all our old schools, colleges or universities, tends to the ornamental killing of time, let us endeavour to draw the line which separates the useful and necessary of the arts and sciences, from those which are merely ornamental and amusing, that conduce more to the fame of the professor, than to the benefit of the pupil.

The art of drawing or delineation, which has been placed (because its utility was not well understood) amongst the fine arts, must be ranked amongst those which are useful, as it is probably the most expeditious, correct, easy and pleasant mode, of giving ideas both to children and adults. Representation is the only defined language, and is perhaps equal in value and utility to all the languages together; without it, we can have no correct idea of mechanics or natural history; when the objects themselves are absent, descriptions, from the undefined nature of words, must be equally vague and uncertain. An idea is a representation in the mind of a thing thought of; but let any one try to represent to himself a machine, animal, plant, mineral, or any complicated body from a description, and he will find the great difficulty and in most cases the impossibility of imprinting a correct figure on his mind, without which he cannot have a correct idea of the thing thought of. No exact idea of a visual object can be obtained, without an equally exact figure in the mind; what does not come by the senses, cannot be figured in the mind, of course cannot be called a correct idea, but must remain vague and imperfect.

CHEMISTRY, like all other sciences is only useful to the individual as far as he is likely to practise it, such as that of the kitchen and wash-house, of food and cleanliness, two of the most indispensable operations of life, of soap-boiling, candle-making, and dying, with all applications to any of the useful arts, agriculture, &c. The higher branches of speculative analysis, ought to be left to those qualifying themselves for professors. Where is the necessity of knowing the properties of substances, that you never will come in contact with, or from which you will never require any aid or assistance, and what the utility of learning a complete course of chemistry, if, for want of practice, it will be forgotten, as it usually is, in a very few years?

NATURAL HISTORY, or a knowledge of all the useful properties of animate and inanimate bodies that nature has placed round us, is highly useful in education; instructs us in the various uses we can make of them, and leads us to acquire the habit of investigation; while the pleasure children take in such an examination is so gratifying to their curiosity, as totally to supercede the necessity of coercion and consequently the creating any species of fear as a motive of action,—fear, the dreadful enemy to human happiness, that cancer of the mind, that unceasing torment through all its innumerable ramifications. For these and many other reasons that might be adduced, the different branches of natural history, ought perhaps to be the foundation on which instruction is bottomed, as consisting of simple ideas obtained by the direct exercise of the senses.

MINERALOGY, or the properties of the different substances that cover the surface of our part of the globe, (for the investigation of the properties of matter existing at thousands of leagues from us, with which we have no necessary connection, is not immediately useful to us) ought to be the first, and perhaps the only subject, of children's instruction. The properties of the different kinds of clay, which are fit for brick-making, furnaces, crucibles, potters, &c. &c., with the mode of testing them; the properties of the different kinds of sands for moulding, glass-making, &c.; the properties of the different kinds of limestones when burned, for manure, mortar, &c. &c.; of the different kinds of rocks for building, road-making, &c. &c., and the modes of trying them; and the properties and uses of different kinds of metals, &c., the limiting all those researches to substances within their reach, and which they will probably have to work or use in the course of some necessary occupation, are the proper subjects of investigation for the young student. For this purpose I would recommend a cabinet to be collected by the youth themselves; in proportion as they are taught the names and qualities of minerals, gathering a few during every ramble they may take, and learning how to break specimens, accommodated to the drawers of their cabinet; they should then test their hardness, &c. to render them familiar with all their external properties, and this should be so often reiterated that they could not possibly forget them. The properties of minerals useful in the arts, which come from abroad, might be next studied; but the 99-100ths of the elegant cabinets, collected at immense expense by connoisseurs, consisting of rare beautiful crystals, which are seldom found, (for as Delomeux used to say, "you may travel 500 leagues without meeting with a crystal,") are only for the brilliant display of the industry and fame of the owner, but of no practical use either to him or any one else. Teaching by one of those valuable cabinets that consist of some thousands of specimens, is equally nugatory; when 30 or 40 specimens are passed rapidly before the pupils, too elegant to be handled or any of their external characters tried, the recollection of them vanishes from the mind by the time the drawer which contained them is replaced; so that even supposing the knowledge of them could be put to any practical use, their great variety, and rapidity with which they run round the circle of students, render all positive knowledge of them almost impossible; even the curiosity of the student is not sufficiently awakened by the apparent utility of the study, to tempt him to recur to it as a future employment, or even amusement, and in a few years the labors of the school vanish like smoke.

Geology is the application of mineralogy to the relative position of the rocks on the surface of the earth; and though the practice is laborious, and requires much travelling and examination of the different ranges of mountains, yet the theory, as far as regards the usual relative positions of the different classes of rocks, is easy and simple, and may be taught in five lessons as well as in five hundred. Make a circle on a slate to represent the earth, draw a line on the inside to represent the primitive class of rocks, as the foundation of all we know of it, and at the same time expose a drawer with 20 or 30 specimens of primitive rocks accurately ticketed, to the examination of the pupils, who ought to be allowed to test all their properties and to investigate them so thoroughly, as to have their names and qualities so associated together as to recur immediately to the mind on seeing them. This constitutes their first lesson. For the second lesson which might be so many days after the first as to give time for acquiring well a knowledge of all the primitive rocks, draw another line over the first, to represent the transition, and expose 30 or 40 specimens of transition rocks, also accurately ticketed, a sufficient time for minute examination. Draw another line over the transition to represent the secondary, for the third lesson, and display 40 or 50 specimens for the inspection of the pupils, as in the former classes. For the fourth lesson, a line over the secondary, for the alluvial with 10 or 20 specimens for the inspection of the pupils, as in former classes. The fifth lesson shows the volcanic rocks, which alternate indiscriminately with the three last classes of what have been called Neptunian rocks; 50 or 60 specimens of this class, should be submitted to the inspection of the pupils, as in the other classes.

This regular super-position of strata, does not exist now on the whole surface of the earth, but in some places all that is here represented over the primitive, either has never been laid there or has been removed by some accident or convulson of nature, presenting the primitive at the surface; the same with the transition and secondary. Experience has not yet produced any well-attested facts of the relative position of the different classes being reversed, in any place where they are all found; that is, the transition in its natural state always lays over the primitive, the secondary always over the transition, &c.

The most difficult class to distinguish accurately from the others, is the transition, and it would perhaps be the shortest way of teaching geology, to begin by ascertaining what is transition; as the primitive under it and the

Opinions on Various Subjects 237

secondary over it, are so different in structure, component parts, &c. as not to be mistaken.

BOTANY is perhaps the science wherein language is best defined, yet it is difficult for a student seeking the description of a plant in a book, to find its generic and specific name. It is probable, that a knowledge of the application of the scientific language sufficient to enable them to find out the name by finding the description of a plant, is all that is either useful or necessary for any of the millions to acquire. To accomplish this, a botanical dictionary and the description of the plants of the country is all that is wanted; commencing with the nature and properties of all the plants in the garden, proceeding from that to the fields and surrounding woods; beginning in the spring, and collecting the flowers every day as they come out, imprinting the name on the mind, so associated with the plant that it would occur on seeing it—this might be a recreation one hour in the day, until all the plants in the neighborhood were completely known. A botanic garden might be made in this country at little or no expense, by enclosing an acre or two of the woods and transplanting all the different species found in the vicinity into it. There are very few of the thousand plants found on the surface of the earth, that men have yet learned how to make use of. The knowledge of all the others that have not been applied to useful purposes, must be considered as amusement and pastime, which may safely be deferred, until circumstances, into which the man may be thrown, prove the necessity of such a mode of spending time. To instruct the millions in the most genteel, elegant or agreeable mode of amusing themselves, may not suit either their convenience or inclination, and must be at best premature.

The immense luxurious expense of hot-houses, greenhouses, &c.; of transporting plants from the equator towards the poles, to pamper the few with vegetables forced by artificial heat out of the climate, is perhaps a misapplication of both time and labor. But the slow and gradual transportation of useful vegetables from the south to the north on this continent, by moving them, a plantation at a time, up the banks of the Mississippi, or any other of our rivers that run north and south, may be an easy and cheap means of increasing our comforts, by varying both our food and raiment; as in the instances of the sweet potato, cotton, &c. The few experiments yet judiciously made, warrant a conclusion that the greatest part of the useful vegetables, might be acclimated much farther north than they at present grow, and we may not despair of cultivating the sugar cane as far north as the latitude of 40, though not in the same perfection as our southern neighbors, yet sufficiently so to be more profitable than any other production for making sugar. Plants, as they are freer from bad habits than animals, may be easier accustomed to any climate.

ZOOLOGY, or the nature and properties of animals, may in a useful education, be limited, 1st, to those we use for food: 2nd, those that assist us, when tamed, in the different necessary operations, our wants (multiplied by civilization) require, and 3d, all those that from their instinct are led to prey on our property. The two first have attracted the attention of mankind from time immemorial; the last, though not the least interesting, have been much neglected, perhaps because a great portion of them are so minute, innumerable and so secreted and disguised as to escape common observation,—I mean the depredatory insects.—Any invention or operation that could prevent their immense increase, or destroy them when in existence, would be a great benefit, and the greater the number of those that study their habits, nature, and the places where they breed, the greater the probability of finding out some cure or protection, against the depredations: the more extensive the diffusion of that knowledge amongst the great mass of productive laborers, who from the situation they are placed in have more opportunities of being acquainted with their haunts, the greater the probability of discovering a remedy.

ARITHMETIC by head or memory, without the aid of cyphers, and best taught by the aid of an instrument called an arithmometer, before the child knows the value of cyphers, is the true discipline for all the mental faculties, as it exercises, improves and accelerates combination,—renders comparison easy and accurate—accustoms the young mind to rapid deductions, facilitates the drawing of just and accurate conclusions,—and lays the foundation for a quick, impartial and logical judgment, in deciding on all questions of intricacy and difficulty, by furnishing to the mind the necessary elements to unravel the most complicated subjects. For these reasons it is a fit companion to go hand in hand with natural history, which exercises and sharpens all the senses, teaches the necessity of accurate and minute investigation, practises the most pleasant mode of analysis, and forms the judgment regarding surrounding objects on the solid basis of experience. It is best taught by the objects themselves, or accurate representations of them, the best descriptions leaving on the mind only a vague and indefinite idea.

MECHANISM, that injector of mind into matter, for the use of man, which substitutes the ingenious organization of inert substances, in the place of manual labor, furthers the progress of real civilization, perhaps more than any thing else. It is more than probable, that the knowledge of subduing matter to the use of man, ought to be the foundation of all useful civilization, and the people who begin otherwise, begin at the wrong end. The study of the simple mechanical powers, such as the lever, screw, pully, &c., progressing gradually towards the more complicated calculation of wheel work and the application of geometry to all kinds of mill work, the power of running water and practical Hydraulics, are all to be learned by careful examination of the machines themselves, or models or accurate representations of them. The simplest machinery ought to be studied first, such as the most perfect implements of husbandry and of all the useful arts. The more complicated, for manufactories, such as for spinning and weaving cotton and wool, the construction of the most improved steam engines, &c., being more difficult, ought to be learned after the more simple; but as all mechanism has been contrived as our wants required, it must therefore be considered as all useful and necessary to the occupations of man, and must be learnt in the order of their utility, depending on the situation and locality of the individual, and leaving to the last those inventions which are purely ornamental or for the facilitating of luxury, until surrounding circumstances prove, that it is convenient or within their reach to indulge in such superfluities. Mechanism by its nature being removed from all the delusions of fancy, caprice or imagination, as well as its useful applications to most of the occupations of man, ought to be the solid foundation on which is built the future happiness and prosperity of mankind.

MATHEMATICS.—Geometry, plain Trigonometry, practical Geometry, with the common rules of land mensuration and navigation, are all the millions can ever have use for in this branch of science. Spherical trigonometry, fluxions, &c., not one in one hundred thousand has the smallest occasion to use after leaving school. Ninety-nine hundredths of Euclid, which has been so much esteemed as the best discipline to correct reasoning, is entirely forgotten by the same proportion of those who get it by rote, which is the only way it can be got at the time it is taught to youths as the grammar of mathematics, before they can comprehend one application of it to practice. It has occurred in this back country, that two or three professors of mathematics were forced to apply to a back-woods man to run a line by the compass, and measure a field; so distant are the school theories from the practice, in almost all sciences.

In NATURAL PHILOSOPHY, some of the useful properties of the fluids that surround us, such as light, heat, air, water, electricity, galvanism, magnetism, &c., are all that the mass of mankind will have occasion to make use of, together with the common laws of motion and gravitation, as applied to mechanism, without any speculation on the cause; for the effects are perhaps the only part of both morals and physics that interest us. What an immensity of the energy of intellect has been thrown away in endeavours to conjecture the nature of causes, that must be for ever hid from beings so constructed as we are, and to what a sophistical change of reasoning has the catenation of the two words, cause and effect, given rise!

GEOGRAPHY.—The use of the globes to show the form of the earth, with some of the large divisions, and perhaps the minute divisions of one's own country, may be sometimes useful; though it is probable, that every thing that can be accurately ascertained by referring to a map or statistical table, is only an unnecessary burthen to the memory, of knowledge that may or may not be useful, according to the circumstances of the parties; and when positively useful, few can depend so implicitly on their memory, as to dispense with a map or statistical tables. The discrimination of north from south and east from west, for the latitude and longitude (though a knowledge the famous ancients were totally ignorant of) is all that is necessary for the examination of a map.

ASTRONOMY.—In this science, a knowledge of the diurnal motion of the earth to explain the rising and setting of the sun, moon and stars, with the annual movement round the sun, to explain the cause of the different seasons, and of the planetary system, with the cause of the moon's phases, all of which ought to be taught by figures or an orrery, is full as much as can be useful to mankind in general.

To all those who would have any thing to do with building houses, a few of the principles of architecture may be necessary, as well as naval architecture to such as are likely to freight or own ships.

Literature very properly called Belles Letters, perhaps from the beauty of the letter and the harmony of the sound, including its principal properties, is at best an ornament, that all language which conveys useful information, can easily dispense with. The flowers of rhetoric and declamation, only serve to disguise the truth and puzzle all who attempt to convert them into common sense. A plain, simple narrative of facts, got by evidence of the senses, is all the literature that 99-100ths of mankind have occasion for, and the thing most to be guarded against, is the exaggerated delusion of the imagination, by attempting to embellish, under pretence of interesting the hearers more in favour of the relater, though in so doing he loses their confidence and his

Opinions on Various Subjects

character as a man of truth, without which no one can maintain the reputation of an honest man, who, as Pope says, is the "noblest work of God." To begin by literature before the mind has acquired ideas, is like attempting to polish a sponge, and it is more than probable, that the attention and industry necessary to secure correct ideas, will furnish appropriate language to convey the ideas to another, which is all that a reasonable being ought to require. When we cannot explain our meaning to another, it is not generally for want of language, but because the idea is vague and undefined; diluting it in an ocean of words will only add to difficulty. The laconism of the French notarial language, constitutes its merit as a clear and defined medium of registering contracts.

It is probable that every biped dreams when asleep, and improbable that all other animals do the same; but our species is perhaps the only one that dreams when awake; that allow their imagination to run riot with their thoughts and build castles in the air, resembling nothing in existence, though the different parts came to them through the medium of their senses; for we can figure nothing in our minds, of which the component parts were not received by our senses; any other idea would be innate, which has been exploded.

The vast variety of metaphysical, the theological, and earthly dreams, that torment or amuse mankind, would fill some hundred or perhaps some thousand volumes; there are no bounds to imagination when unlimited by facts. The two first mentioned kind of dreams, are as far beyond any possibility of estimating their numbers, as they are beyond the comprehension of beings constituted like men. The earthly dreams have seized upon a part of all the sciences; form the principal materials of all the different religions; constitute the quackery of all professions, and the ingredients that make dupes of the ignorant by the cunning of the knowing. In alchemy, it was the philosopher's stone that made their dream; even our modern chemists are not quite purged of the effects of a heated imagination, in spite of the crucible. The conjecture how nature made the earth, without any proof of its ever having been made, is the geological dream; the spontaneous creation of animals, by beginning with the most simple and finishing with the most compound, is the Zoological dream; plurality of worlds is one of the astronomical dreams; funds, land and bank speculation, originated in a legion of dreams, in this country, the result of which is far from being yet decided; the mercantile field of dreaming was so extended during our neutral trade, that many are yet bewildered so as to doubt the evidence of their senses; the fatal dream of the south-sea-bubble, and Law's bank at Paris, did not prevent our legislatures from giving all our banks the same charter. Our Indians, when they want any thing from you, dream that you gave it them, which is the only advantage got from dreaming. The great source of all our civilized dreams is the immense pains taken at all our schools, in cultivating the imagination at the expense of the judgment; not satisfied with our own absurd fancies, the heads of our youth are stuffed full of ancient mythology, and our school books filled with Roman and Grecian dreams, held forth as models of eloquence and taste.

Of all the animals, man is the only one that is ashamed of the form of his own body, out of which arises something of false pride and the greatest part of false delicacy; causes us to imagine the idlest, most useless and too often corrupt actions of humanity, to be the most

Opinions on Various Subjects

meritorious, honourable and respectable. An exaggerated sentiment in females, causes them to tremble at the death of insects, while regarding the real miseries of their fellow-beings with sang froid; they are shocked at the indelicacy of a word, or the name of an indispensable piece of clothing, while looking on actions fraught with cruelty both to man and animals, with the greatest indifference, and even with pleasure. There is nothing too absurd or contradictory for the imagination, supported by fashion, to adopt; when we abandon utility as the scale of value, we are adrift on the sea of caprice, fancy and whim, without either rudder or compass. The time between infancy and youth and age, is too long (in our state of habitual indolence and aversion from tracing effects up to their causes) for us to observe the origin of 9-10ths of our fixed habits, which are stamped upon us when children, while the physical as well as the moral, is soft and pliable to all impression. We therefore continue our mode of thinking and acting, without reflecting how great a proportion of our ideas, manners, habits and customs, were instilled into us before the age of reason: and the follies of the nursery and the school, fill the gray head of the dotard, who returns to childhood when society have the greatest reverence and confidence in him.

There is frailty in imagining ones self above all that surrounds us, which young ignorant people proclaim to all the world, by a supercilious impudent look and strut, as if they would trample every one under their feet. It is the great mistake of ignorance; they ought always to be modest, and avoid drawing the attention of others to criticise their foibles. It is further a proof that they are not only ignorant, but that they are so far deficient in understanding as not to have the least knowledge of their own weakness, and of course never take the trouble, to acquire any information to amend either their moral or physical defects.

The want of good habits, of a healthy, useful and productive occupation, is the origin of a great many of the evils and miseries of life. Such habits can only be lasting and durable, when acquired during the period from infancy to youth, and it is more than probable, they cannot be instilled too early into the soft and pliable disposition of children. The formation of good habits is one of the good effects to be expected from the adoption of Infant Schools.

One of the most injurious effects of the old artificial system of education, as I call it to distinguish it from the Pestalozzian method, which may be denominated the natural system, is the imprisoning of children for four or five hours in the day, to a task of irksome and disgusting study, which nothing but the fear of punishment, could force them to perform; after which they are let loose on society for eight hours, full of revenge and retaliation against their jailors, exerting all their ingenuity to do mischief indiscriminately to all older than themselves, from considering them all as accessary to their persecution and confinement. This, the history of all old academies, and colleges, will sufficiently prove, the number and violence of the rebellious riots and mutinies in Europe as well as in this country, being in exact proportion to the rigor and strictness of their restraints and confinement. The destruction of other's property, is the smallest part of the damage; the originating, creating, fostering and strengthening all the malevolent passions of hatred, revenge, cruelty, &c., entail upon mankind through future generations an immensity of evils and crimes, which giving an excuse for further pains, pen-

Opinions on Various Subjects

alties, imprisonment and tortures, add to the general demoralization of society and can only be cured by a more rational system of education, which shall prevent the seeds of the violent passions from being sown in the fertile and productive minds of youth.

To rectify, as far as education can, the foregoing evils, the system of Pestalozzi, through all its manipulations is admirably calculated. Having travelled seven summers in Switzerland, and some months of each residing at Pestalozzi's school at Yverdun, I never saw the pupils in or out of school without one of the teachers presiding at their games, &c., all of which were calculated to convey instruction. They were constantly occupied with something useful to themselves or others, from 5 o'clock in the morning to 8 o'clock at night, with the exception of four half hours at meals, at which all the teachers ate with the pupils. Their attention was never fatigued with more than one hour at the same exercise either moral or physical; all was bottomed on free will, by the total exclusion of every species of correction. Their actions were cheerful, energetic and rapidly tending towards the end aimed at. I do not recollect ever to have heard a cry or any demonstration of pain or displeasure, nor even an angry word from either teacher or pupil all the time I lived amongst them. Though I often went out of my road fifty leagues to examine young men taught under this system, I do not remember ever finding one of an ill-natured temper, or bad conduct, of all I saw either in Europe or this country, and I generally found them greatly superior, in all the useful accomplishments, to all those educated by other methods. It is on this practical proof of the great superiority of the system that my confidence in its immense utility to mankind, has been founded, as I do not pretend to be a judge of scholastic exercises without seeing the result. One of the most beneficial consequences, is the pleasure all Pestalozzi's pupils take, in mental labor and study. Agreeable sensation being catenated to intellectual employment from the earliest dawn of reason, it continues to be an ornament through life; and all my experience forces me firmly to believe, that education may, with great ease and pleasure, be so conducted, as to render, by early habits, all the useful and necessary operations of both males and females, a pastime and amusement, converting life itself into a play in spite of the delusion of the imagination.

The great difficulty is to find professors, willing to sacrifice their favorite pursuits to the interest and benefit of their pupils. I do not remember ever to have seen any, except Pestalozzi and his pupils, so enthusiastic as to sacrifice all attachment to money, amusement and even every species of knowledge not necessary to their occupation, concentrating all their amusements in teaching. It is difficult to find an adult that will go further than to be an enthusiast while teaching in the regular hours, considering any further encroachment upon his time as a species of slavery not to be endured.—Teaching must constitute the pleasure and amusement of every one that attempts to propagate the system; all that from previous habits consider the time spent with their pupils as a task, performed because paid for, must fall far short of doing justice to their pupils. A great proportion of the Pestalozzian pupils in Europe are enthusiastic propagators of the system and become teachers. In this country there is not one that I know; whether this arise from the golden dreams of the neutral trade, or the little consideration of teachers in society, I will not decide. Perhaps the greatest improvement that can be effected in education, is to free the pupil as much as possible from dependence on the ipse dixit of the master, by teaching him to derive his knowledge directly from the things themselves, or accurate representations of them. Instruct children to teach themselves by their own observations, which make lasting impressions, and enlist self love to enhance the value of the knowledge acquired. This direct mode of instruction, is entirely free from the delusions of the imagination, or local or individual prejudices, which warp, and too often hide in mystery, the discourses of the professors.

Trace to the source, the cause of a great many of our vices and crimes and it will be found in the want of more agreeable and innocent amusements. What else induces the drunkard or gambler to waste his time at the expense of both health and purse? what else prompts all the fashionable killers of time, begets ennui and often ends in suicide? I never knew a natural historian either a drunkard or a gambler, rarely wasting his time on any of the trifling, fashionable amusements, because the immense variety of nature, furnishes him with constant pleasure, benefiting both his health and his pecuniary independence.

The folly of neglecting education cannot be exceeded by that of an architect attempting to build a house without a foundation; and the making education consist of words and sounds, is equal to the absurdity of building a house of paper. The opinion generally spread, of the immense difficulty of giving knowledge to children, must originate in the old system of teaching complex ideas before the simple ones of which they are composed; of teaching to children the grammar, before they understand any other part of a language, and other similar absurdities; which is truly like forcing the butt end of knowledge against the pupils, in place of the pointed end, as in the Pestalozzian method.

The abuse of terms, and vague and uncertain meaning of words, have been among the principal supports of all quackery, both of church and state, and would require a new dictionary to expose them all. One of the most injurious ideas to the well being of society, is the opinion of the old school, that learning is synonymous with knowledge; that the arrangement of words is the same as a correct knowledge of things; that a smattering of the dead language, (out of which not one practical truth can be drawn,) leads to perfection, profit and preferment; and that there is a catenation of sounds or words, one link of which being wanting, the two ends are useless. "Drink deep or taste not the Pierean spring," says Pope; as if the knowledge of a number of plants, minerals, &c., is of no use, if you do not know the whole that are to be found on earth; as if "half a loaf were not better than no bread." Such a delusion could only originate in supposing the harmony of literature, to include all perfection and the smallest stop or obstruction, a discord that would ruin the whole.

While travelling in Europe, having observed how nearly some establishments in Switzerland, &c. were enabled to educate, feed and clothe children, by the produce of their own labor, in a country where land is one hundred times dearer than in this country, and labor for one sixth of our price, the idea suggested itself of the great facility of accomplishing such a plan here. Circumstances beyond my control, have hitherto prevented the trial; but conceiving my present situation favorable for such an experiment, I shall attempt it.—It is more than probable, by the old spelling and horn-book system of five or six years learning to read or write, and eight or

Opinions on Various Subjects

nine years on Latin and Greek, it would be impossible to make children productive either to themselves or others. The adoption of some system of education, limited to the useful, omitting all the speculative and ornamental, is positively necessary to the success of such an undertaking.—The hints given in my former essays, may perhaps suggest ideas that can be practically improved upon, by some whose situation, abilities and experience, fit them better for so useful an undertaking.

The tyranny of the strongest over the weakest has been manifested in all states of society, even where civilization has made some progress. The women are prevented, by the oppression of men, from being so useful either to themselves or others, as they would be, if freed from the arbitrary control of those who are only superior to them in physical strength. The improvement of mankind, has lost the aid and assistance of half the population, by the education of women being confined to their physical accomplishments, and their mental faculties so much neglected. Nearly one half of the utility of men is lost to society, by keeping children so long in leading-strings, without the power of benefiting either themselves or others. Full half of the necessary and useful occupations of life at present monopolized by men, could be better executed by the nimble fingers, and active, flexible hands of women and children. Besides the profit to society, the immense diminution of scandal, malice and disputes, by occupation of females, and the reduction of mischievous destruction by the constant occupation of children would be a great gain. For the most effectual way of keeping them from doing harm either to themselves or others, is to keep them constantly occupied; as idleness is very often the mother of crime, and is always both father and mother of mischief. As "a sensible mother makes a sensible child," perhaps the easiest mode of improving mankind would be to give women a useful education on all points their progeny might have occasion for during their life; for the mothers sow the seeds of every thing that is good, as well as every thing that is bad, in the minds of their offspring. They are the first, and ought to be qualified to be the best, instructors. The ultimate effects, expected by the friends of the Pestalozzian method, were, that as soon as all fathers and mothers were educated by it, their children would not have use for any teacher but their parents, who are the natural instructors according to the natural method.

To multiply and exaggerate the difficulties to be encountered in teaching all the arts and sciences, would appear to be one of the great objects of all masters and professors; it is an egotism so perfectly consistent with the principle of all commerce and trade, to buy cheap and sell dear, that it ought to be expected; what else could induce a continuance of the old system of retaining an apprentice seven years, to learn to make a pair of shoes or sew a coat, keeping a poor child five or six years, tormented with a spelling book? All trades have an interest in enhancing the value of the articles they deal in, and school-masters have no other way of increasing their consequence, than by giving sparingly, the knowledge they possess, to their pupils, and retaining them as long under their tutorage as possible, which both adds to their consideration and purse. I have known many a school-master, turned off by the superiors for advancing too quickly, and heard some declare, that if they could give the knowledge in an Encyclopedia, to their scholars, in one year, they would not; it is exceedingly mortifying to their self-conceit and vanity, to see others arrive at the same quantum of knowledge in

Opinions on Various Subjects

one tenth of the time and with half the labor, they took to acquire it. Alexander the Great's preceptor informed his pupil that he was going to write a book on mathematics; "you will give every one as much knowledge as you gave me;" "no," answered the Preceptor, "I shall take care to make the book in such a manner that they will not get much knowledge out of it." One would be tempted to think that a great many book-makers, follow that example of Alexander's preceptor. "Make the goods to suit the customer," is an old manufacturing adage, which must, with books as with every thing else, vacillate with the caprice and fancy of ignorance, until *cui bono* or *quid utile* be the test applied to every thing.

The art of drawing or delineating, may be learned by tracing the figure from the natural object; or by drawing from a figure, or representation in a print or picture. The first is the most useful, the other is only a copy of what has been already done. A print can be repeated, for a few cents, as often as you please, more accurately than the best draftsman can possibly do. The drawing from the object itself therefore probably is the most useful mode. Substituting a long tedious process of copying, in place of a short expeditious mode by the copperplate press, would be losing the benefit of that admirable invention. Learning to draw from the objects, instructs equally well to delineate from the print or representation; but drawing from the print gives little or no facility in drawing from the object; so that there is double the time and labor spent; which is, perhaps, the reason, that in all drawing schools the pupils are kept copying prints, with the certainty of being obliged afterwards, by as much time and labor, to learn how to represent the natural object. This may be for the interest of the master, but certainly is against the interest of the pupil. Query, whose interest has been consulted in all our old school operations?

Attention is the only medium through which instruction passes into the mind; without it, nothing makes a lasting impression on any of the mental faculties. Can undivided attention be secured by fear or coercion? This is a query necessary to be solved, as a principal upon which education must be bottomed. Does not fear brutalize and paralyze all the faculties of the mind? Let any one at a mature age, reflect on his feelings when under the impression of fear and he will find that neither his memory, judgment, nor any other of his mental faculties, were sound. Fear perhaps is the great predisposing cause of many both moral and physical diseases.

If fear has so debilitating an influence upon the physical and moral qualities of men hardened and strengthened by practice and experience, how much more must its baleful influence pervert and deteriorate the young and tender minds of children? In a state of fear the attention is distracted, and cannot act in unison with the subject taught, and is not secured by good will arising out of the pleasure and amusement children take in an exercise that interests them. If this is so, and my experience does not permit me to doubt it, the essential business and duty of a teacher, is to find out the inclination of his pupils, and teach them any and all the useful lessons he may find they study with pleasure. From the apish disposition of all young children, this is not a hard task; for they are inclined to imitate all the useful operations of life, and are never better pleased, than when their labors are either useful to themselves or to others even in this fashionable, perverted age, where every thing appears to be shameful and disgraceful, in proportion to its utility.

Opinions on Various Subjects

The grand object of all beings is happiness, and the principal aim of every species of education, ought to be to put the youth on the straight road to the goal that all are pushing for, though by various and contrary roads. Misery must be the consequence of the inability to satisfy any of the physical appetites, and the occupation that secures the moderate gratification of those appetites, must be the most useful, because removing the greatest of all obstructions to the enjoyment of happiness, and ought to be the first in the scale of utility, and respectability, as they were in the beginning of the Roman nation, and are still in China. Since the refinement of christianity, all is reversed, and agriculture is become the meanest, most disreputable and worst paid of all the useful arts. Men and things seem to be valued in exact proportion to their uselessness, and various immoral plans, schemes and intrigues to wrest the products of his labor from the productive laborer, (who has to feed and support the useless and non-productive) constitute the most immoral feature of society, and herein originate the greatest part of the evils and crimes that torment humanity. In slave countries it is a perpetual war between force and fraud. In countries where personal liberty exists, the theory is masked by laws, charters, corporations, monopolies, and every contrivance of church and state, to disguise the practice, which all tend to the same end, that of feeding the idle and non-productives. Knowledge is power, says the learned Bacon. Hint to a man in power, the possibility of giving knowledge cheap, and you alarm him, by advocating a plan that would deprive him of the greatest part of his power; and acting upon his own interest (and it would be foolish to expect otherwise,) he cannot do otherwise than oppose your reform with all his might. Nothing else creates the violent opposition to all reform of the old, absurd mode of education. It is not that every one who echoes those opinions, has penetration enough to foresee the consequences; but their vile leaders, from whom they take their opinions, have anticipated the result and adapt their reasoning to the ignorance and prejudices of their dupes, without once hinting at the real motive that actuates themselves.

JOHN F. C. HARRISON received his M.A. from Cambridge University in 1946 and his Ph.D. from Leeds University in 1955. Before joining the faculty of the University of Wisconsin in 1961 as Professor of History, he was Lecturer in History at the University of Leeds and later served as Deputy Director of Adult Education and Extra-Mural Studies there. Professor Harrison's writings include *History of the Working Men's College, 1854–1954* (1954); *Social Reform in Victorian Leeds: James Hole, 1820–1895* (1954); *Learning and Living, 1780–1960* (1961); and *Quest for the New Moral World: Robert Owen and the Owenites in Britain and America* (1968).